MARIJUANA
Mind-Altering Weed

ILLICIT AND MISUSED DRUGS

Abusing Over-the-Counter Drugs:
Illicit Uses for Everyday Drugs

Addiction in America:
Society, Psychology, and Heredity

Addiction Treatment: Escaping the Trap

Alcohol Addiction: Not Worth the Buzz

Cocaine: The Rush to Destruction

Dual Diagnosis: Drug Addiction and Mental Illness

Ecstasy: Dangerous Euphoria

Hallucinogens: Unreal Visions

Heroin and Other Opioids:
Poppies' Perilous Children

Inhalants and Solvents: Sniffing Disaster

Marijuana: Mind-Altering Weed

Methamphetamine: Unsafe Speed

Natural and Everyday Drugs:
A False Sense of Security

Painkillers: Prescription Dependency

Recreational Ritalin: The Not-So-Smart Drug

Sedatives and Hypnotics: Deadly Downers

Steroids: Pumped Up and Dangerous

Tobacco: Through the Smoke Screen

ILLICIT AND MISUSED DRUGS

MARIJUANA
Mind-Altering Weed

By E. J. Sanna

Mason Crest

Mason Crest
370 Reed Road
Broomall, Pennsylvania 19008
www.masoncrest.com

Printed in the Hashemite Kingdom of Jordan.

First printing
9 8 7 6 5 4 3 2 1

Library of Congress Cataloging-in-Publication Data

Sanna, E. J.
Marijuana : mind-altering weed / E.J. Sanna.
    p. cm. — (Illicit and misused drugs)
Includes bibliographical references and index.
ISBN 978-1-4222-2435-9 (hardcover)
ISBN 978-1-4222-2454-0 (paperback)
ISBN 978-1-4222-2424-3 (series hardcover)
ISBN 978-1-4222-9299-0 (ebook)
1. Marijuana—Juvenile literature. 2. Marijuana abuse—Juvenile literature. I. Title.
  HV5822.M3S366 2012
  362.29'5—dc23
                                        2011032569

Interior design by Benjamin Stewart.
Cover design by Torque Advertising + Design.
Produced by Harding House Publishing Services, Inc.
www.hardinghousepages.com

This book is meant to educate and should not be used as an alternative to appropriate medical care. Its creators have made every effort to ensure that the information presented is accurate—but it is not intended to substitute for the help and services of trained professionals.

CONTENTS

Introduction   6
1. What Is Marijuana?   9
2. The History of Marijuana   19
3. Who Uses Marijuana?   33
4. What Are the Dangers of Marijuana?   43
5. What Are the Legal Consequences of Using
    Marijuana?   65
6. Controversial Issues   81
7. Treatment   109

Glossary   119
Further Reading   121
For More Information   122
Bibliography   123
Index   125
Picture Credits   127
Author/Consultant Biographies   128

INTRODUCTION

Addicting drugs are among the greatest challenges to health, well-being, and the sense of independence and freedom for which we all strive—and yet these drugs are present in the everyday lives of most people. Almost every home has alcohol or tobacco waiting to be used, and has medicine cabinets stocked with possibly outdated but still potentially deadly drugs. Almost everyone has a friend or loved one with an addiction-related problem. Almost everyone seems to have a solution neatly summarized by word or phrase: medicalization, legalization, criminalization, war-on-drugs.

For better and for worse, drug information seems to be everywhere, but what information sources can you trust? How do you separate misinformation (whether deliberate or born of ignorance and prejudice) from the facts? Are prescription drugs safer than "street" drugs? Is occasional drug use really harmful? Is cigarette smoking more addictive than heroin? Is marijuana safer than alcohol? Are the harms caused by drug use limited to the users? Can some people become addicted following just a few exposures? Is treatment or counseling just for those with serious addiction problems?

These are just a few of the many questions addressed in this series. It is an empowering series because it provides the information and perspectives that can help people come to their own opinions and find answers to the challenges posed by drugs in their own lives. The series also provides further resources for information and assistance, recognizing that no single source has all the answers. It should be of interest and relevance to areas of study spanning biology, chemistry, history, health, social studies, and more. Its efforts to provide a real-world context for the information that is clearly presented but not overly simplified should be appreciated by students, teachers, and parents.

The series is especially commendable in that it does not pretend to pose easy answers or imply that all decisions can be made on the basis of simple facts: some challenges have no immediate or simple solutions, and some solutions will need to rely as much upon basic values as basic facts. Despite this, the series should help to at least provide a foundation of knowledge. In the end, it may help as much by pointing out where the solutions are not simple, obvious, or known to work. In fact, at many points, the reader is challenged to think for him- or herself by being asked what his or her opinion is.

A core concept of the series is to recognize that we will never have all the facts, and many of the decisions will never be easy. Hopefully, however, armed with information, perspective, and resources, readers will be better prepared for taking on the challenges posed by addictive drugs in everyday life.

— *Jack E. Henningfield, Ph.D.*

1 What Is Marijuana?

Alby's problems started on a summer day in Yonkers, New York, when he was thirteen. "You need to get your mind right. Hit this blunt," a friend told him while they were hanging out on the street. (A blunt is a cigar hollowed out and refilled with either marijuana or a mix of cocaine and marijuana.) Alby didn't want to tell his friend no; it seemed rude, and he wanted people to like him. He felt he had to smoke the blunt to fit in.

It wasn't like his parents had taught him anything different. They were drug addicts who couldn't handle the demands of parenting, so Alby had bounced from a foster home to his grandmother's house to a group home. Then, when Alby was fourteen, his mother died. It just didn't seem fair to Alby that his life was so messed up. "I had a grudge against the world," he admitted to the National Institute on Drug Abuse (NIDA).

After he used marijuana for the first time, Alby was convinced: marijuana was cool. He kept on using the drug because he liked the feeling it gave him. "It had me

Other Names for Marijuana

grass	weed	skunk
dope	gear	hash
draw	ganja	hashish
puff	herb	pot
blow	wacky baccy	Mary Jane

in another state of mind," he said. "I was relaxed. All my problems seemed like they were disappearing." Alby's problems really weren't disappearing, of course. Actually, they were getting worse, because the good feelings marijuana gave him came at a price.

Over the next five years, Alby smoked marijuana every day, several times a day. He went to school high, which had a huge impact on his ability to pay attention in class. He wasn't learning anything, his grades plummeted, and eventually he dropped out. "I was losing focus. My attention went from 100 to 0. I was depressed," he said in the interview with NIDA.

But Alby kept on smoking marijuana. In fact, he would do most anything to get high. Marijuana isn't free, so eventually, he started dealing drugs to pay for his habit. He ended up in Valhalla Correctional Facility, a maximum-security jail in Westchester County.

Since then, Alby has made some changes in his life. Counseling has helped him sort out his problems. He has a new group of friends, and he is working on building himself a better life. He'd like to be a mechanic.

But he still feels some of the effects of his drug use. "Sometimes I want to say things, and I can't get them out. I can't find the words," Alby said. "I never had that problem before I started smoking. I used to know things, but now, it's rusty. I forgot how to do division."

Smoking marijuana can become the focal point of a user's day. Everything can center on getting and using the drug.

Teens and Marijuana

New research is giving us better insight into the serious consequences of teen marijuana use, especially how it may impact mental health.

- Young people who use marijuana weekly have double the risk of depression later in life.
- Teens ages twelve through seventeen who smoke marijuana weekly are three times more likely than nonusers to have suicidal thoughts.
- There is evidence of increased risk for schizophrenia in later years in some teens who smoke marijuana.

The Teen Brain

A teen brain is different than an adult brain in many ways. High schoolers, for instance, tend to love things and love them intensely. Teens tend to make decisions based on their emotions rather than reason. That's because the limbic system, the area that controls memory and emotions, is highly developed in a teenager, while the prefrontal cortex, the area responsible for judgment, is still developing.

Certain brain centers, such as the limbic system, are highly influenced by THC (tetrahydrocannabinol), the active ingredient in marijuana. This means the same centers responsible for memory formation, emotion, aggression and fear are also the ones significantly affected by pot.

(Source: National Youth Anti-Drug Media Campaign)

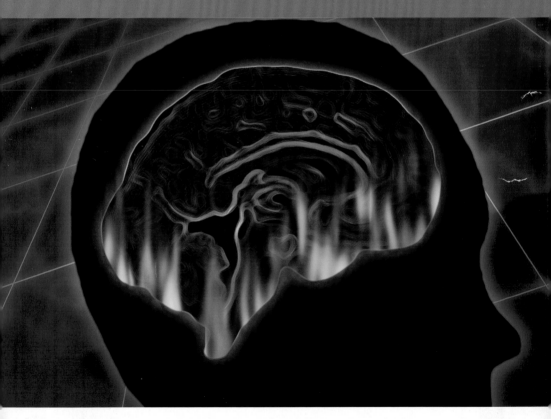

Drugs affect the brain in many ways. Teens may feel emotions more intensely, and memory loss can occur.

Alby's memory problems may get better eventually. And his future is a whole lot more promising now that he's off marijuana.

With a reputation for being used by teenagers and hippies, marijuana is often considered to be a relatively mild drug. However, marijuana, as Alby found out, can lead to serious consequences, just like any other drug.

Where Does Marijuana Come From?

Marijuana, like many other illicit drugs, originates from a plant. *Cannibis Sativa*, or hemp, is dried, and the parts of the plant—everything from the leaves to the flowers and seeds—are used as a hallucinogen. This mixture of organic parts can be various colors, but for the most part, they vary between shades of green, gray, and brown. While marijuana is the most common drug that derives from the hemp plant, other stronger drugs come from the same origin; hashish and sinsemilla are both more potent varieties of the same drug.

Is Marijuana Addiction Genetic?

Studies have found that heredity often influences the user's chance of having a good or bad high. One particular study compared the responses of marijuana use in identical and fraternal twins. The identical twins, which share all of the same genes, were more likely to have the same response to the drug.

The same study, however, showed that the family environment did not contribute at all to people's response to marijuana. In other words, people who grew up in unstable or abusive homes are no more likely to turn to marijuana than are people from stable households. Instead, factors like the availability of the drug, peer pressure, and expectations do affect the response to the drug.

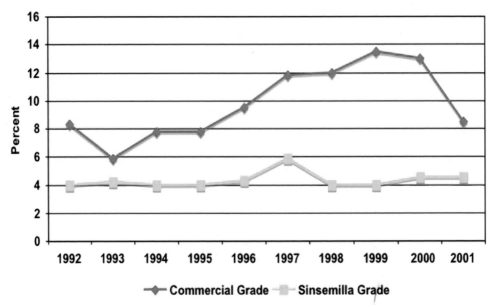

Marijuana Potency (1992–2001)

Trends in the potency of marijuana (and its cousin, sinsemilla) have changed over time.

Like cigarettes and many other addictive drugs, marijuana does not contain just one single chemical. While more than 400 different substances can be found in one joint, the most common chemical is delta-9-tetrahydrocannabinol, or THC. The amount of THC determines how strong the marijuana is: the more of this chemical in the drug, the more potent it is. This amount has been steadily increasing since the 1970s, meaning that the pot smoked thirty years ago was less powerful than what is smoked today. This makes marijuana more dangerous than it used to be; while users experience a stronger high, they also are subject to more possible harmful consequences.

Joints, Bongs, and Blunts

Marijuana is usually smoked in hand-rolled cigarettes called joints. However, other methods for smoking this drug are used as well, including pipes, often called bongs, and cigars called blunts. Blunts are made by taking regular cigars and replacing the tobacco with marijuana; they often contain other drugs as well as marijuana. The most common additive is crack cocaine.

While the most common method of consumption for marijuana is through some kind of smoking, some people brew tea using the leaves of the plant. Sometimes marijuana is mixed with foods, such as brownies.

Method of Action

When marijuana smoke is inhaled or otherwise taken into the body, the fat in the body's organs absorbs the THC. The drug's smoke acts in a similar way to tobacco smoke, passing through the lungs and into the bloodstream. From there it is carried to the organs, the most important of these being the brain.

Once in the brain, the THC connects to specific receptors on nerve cells. These receptors, known as cannabinoid receptors, allow the THC to affect the activities of the cells to which it binds. Each type of nerve cell in the brain has a different number of receptors; some have many, others have few to none. The number of receptors determines which brain functions are affected most by marijuana use and consumption. The majority of the receptors, and therefore where most of the drug's effects are felt, are in the areas of the brain that control memory, concentration and thought, pleasurable feelings, the perception of time and senses, and movement.

Marijuana's ability to impair performance and dramatically increase heart rate is related to the amount of THC contained in the batch of marijuana. This is a

Some people think of marijuana as a symbol of the 1960s, like tie-dyed fabric and the peace sign. But it was used long before then, and continues to be popular.

variable amount, so users may not always be able to predict the effects marijuana will have on them. According to NIDA, marijuana's average THC content increased from 1.08 percent in the 1970s to 5.73 percent in the 2000s.

The smoke of a marijuana joint can contain hundreds of chemicals. It contains particulate matter as well as various substances in gaseous form. In fact, marijuana smoke can be just as harmful as tobacco smoke, as it contains similar amounts of such harmful compounds as carbon monoxide, hydrogen cyanide, and tar. This smoke is what causes the risk of cancer, not the cannabis itself.

Marijuana is often thought of in connection with the hippies and "flower children" of the sixties. A lot of people assume that this was when marijuana use first started. Truth is, though, this drug has been around a whole lot longer.

Cannabineae.

Cannabis sativa L.

W. Muller.

2 The History of Marijuana

The hemp plant has been around for thousands of years. Archaeologists have found hemp fibers that date as far back as 4000 BCE, and cannabis seeds were being used as a food source two thousand years before that. The first recorded use of the marijuana plant dates back to 2737 BCE, when Emperor Shen-Nung of China recommended the plant to treat constipation, "female problems," rheumatism, malaria, *gout*, and "absentmindedness." While he did mention the *hallucinogenic* properties, the medical value was stressed more strongly. From China, the use of the drug as a medicine and recreational hallucinogen spread to India and North Africa. Muslims in these countries used the drug recreationally, partly because while the Koran bans the consumption of alcohol, marijuana use is allowed. Muslims were the first ones to develop hashish, which spread to Iran as well.

In India, marijuana was celebrated as a "divine nectar" that gave people long life and visions of gods. While it was most often used in a *resin* form, there are records of cannabis incense being used around the ninth

Dating Systems and Their Meaning

You might be accustomed to seeing dates expressed with the abbreviations BC or AD, as in the year 1000 BC or the year AD 1900. For centuries, this dating system has been the most common in the Western world. However, since BC and AD are based on Christianity (BC stands for Before Christ and AD stands for *anno Domini*, Latin for "in the year of our Lord"), many people now prefer to use abbreviations that people from all religions can be comfortable using. The abbreviations BCE (meaning Before Common Era) and CE (meaning Common Era) mark time in the same way (for example, 1000 BC is the same year as 1000 BCE, and AD 1900 is the same year as 1900 CE), but BCE and CE do not have the same religious overtones as BC and AD.

Historically, marijuana has been believed to cure almost anything, including leprosy.

century BCE. The plant was claimed to cure such maladies as dandruff, sexually transmitted diseases, *leprosy*, insomnia, and tuberculosis. Even today, many Indian peoples use it medicinally; some groups say that it is effective in treating snakebites, while others use it to ease the pains during childbirth.

Marijuana reached Europe around 500 BCE, where it was used largely medicinally. People distinguished between the different kinds of hemp, citing weedy hemp as being good for curing hard tumors and cultivated hemp as useful for curing things like coughs. However, they also recognized some harmful potential side effects, warning that the plant caused *sterility*.

In 1545, the Spanish brought marijuana to the Americas. Though Native Americans gradually adopted its use, it was not usually used in religious or spiritual ceremonies, as it often was in India.

Marijuana and the Spiritual World

Today, some Indian tribes use hemp for religious rites when the sacred hallucinogenic cactus called peyote is not available. Others, like the groups in the Mexican states of Veracruz, Puebla, and Hidalgo, practice communal ceremonies where the hemp plant is seen as a means of communicating with the Holy Virgin. There, the hemp plant is seen as both the Earth's spirit and the heart of God. Because of this, the plant is both revered and feared. These groups believe the plant to be capable of experiencing feelings in the way a person is, and that it can assume the shape of one's soul.

Why Is Marijuana Dangerous?

- Kids who are regular marijuana users often have shortened attention spans, decreased energy and ambition, lack of judgment, high distractibility, and impaired ability to communicate and relate to others—a set of symptoms psychologists call "amotivational syndrome."

- Kids who regularly smoke marijuana often make risky decisions about driving or having sex.

- Using marijuana can lead to symptoms of depression and thoughts of suicide.

- Regular marijuana use can lead to breathing problems and greater exposure to cancerous chemicals than from tobacco. In fact, one marijuana cigarette can deliver four times as much cancer-causing tar as one tobacco cigarette.

In 1611, the English introduced marijuana as a commercial crop in the colony of Jamestown. There it was used as a source of fiber and was grown along with tobacco for sale back in Europe; this was the first time the plant had been cultivated and grown in large quantities. In Jamestown, it was used for medicine and for fiber; cloth was made from the fibers and made into clothing. However, its popularity did not last long. By 1890, cotton had replaced hemp. While some medicines contained marijuana, the medicinal use of cocaine and opium were much more common.

In the 1920s, Americans rediscovered marijuana, some say because of Prohibition and the laws against consuming alcohol; people looking for oblivion from their troubles turned to a new way of getting high. Mexican workers brought marijuana with them over the border, and the drug spread through the South. While marijuana was not seen as a social threat like alcohol during those years, its use was widely confined to musicians and other people in show business. Songs emerged about "reefer," and "pads"—marijuana clubs—started appearing in cities. Unlike the speakeasies (clubs that featured alcohol), police left marijuana clubs alone, because the people who visited did not become rowdy (like drunks did), and the drug was not illegal.

From 1850 until 1942, the hemp plant was listed in the United States **Pharmacopoeia**. It was said to cure such conditions as labor pains and nausea. However, in the 1930s, the U.S. Federal Bureau of Narcotics (now the U.S. Bureau of Narcotics and Dangerous Drugs)

Peyote has an important role in some Native American rituals. When it's not available, marijuana is sometimes substituted.

began a campaign to show marijuana as a dangerous, addictive, *"gateway drug,"* which it is still considered today.

In 1970, the Controlled Substances Act was passed. This law classified marijuana, along with drugs like LSD and heroin, as a Schedule I drug, meaning that it had a high risk of abuse and no acceptable medicinal use. In 1975, Mexico, America's main source of marijuana, agreed to spray all its marijuana plants with a pesticide. However, this did not stop drug users, who simply turned to Colombia for their supplies.

Throughout the 1980s, marijuana use in the United States declined, mostly because of the war on drugs led by the Ronald Reagan and G. H. W. Bush administrations. Laws were passed that decreased the smuggling of marijuana over the border from Mexico and established *mandatory sentences* for possession. Because of this, dealers stopped buying marijuana from other countries, and small farms designed to grow the highest possible yield started springing up, especially in states like Hawaii and California. In the 1990s, marijuana use again started to increase, especially among young people.

In the Canadian Addiction Survey, conducted by Health Canada and the Canadian Centre in Substance Abuse, it was found that marijuana use among Canadians had almost doubled between 1994 and 2004. However, the Canadian Alcohol and Drug Use Monitoring Survey reported that marijuana use has recently dropped. In 2010, 10.6% of Canadians over 15 had used marijuana, compared with 14.1% in 2004.

Anti-drug policies led to stiffer sentencing guidelines for drug offenses. Increasing numbers of prison and jail cells are occupied by nonviolent drug offenders.

Marijuana—Mind-Altering Weed

Cannabis Time Line:

Marijuana's History Around the World

6000 BCE	Cannabis seeds are used for food in China.
4000 BCE	Textiles made of hemp are used in China.
2727 BCE	First recorded use of cannabis as medicine appears in the Chinese pharmacopoeia.
1500 BCE	Cannabis is cultivated in China for food and fiber.
1500 BCE	Scythians cultivate cannabis and use it to weave fine hemp cloth.
1200–800 BCE	Bhang (dried cannabis leaves, seeds and stems) is mentioned in the Hindu sacred text *Atharva veda* (Science of Charms) as "Sacred Grass," one of the five sacred plants of India. It is used medicinally and ritually as an offering to Shiva.
700–600 BCE	The Zoroastrian Zend-Avesta, an ancient Persian religious text of several hundred volumes allegedly written by Zarathustra (Zoroaster), refers to bhang as Zoroaster's "good narcotic."
700–300 BCE	Scythian tribes leave cannabis seeds as offerings in royal tombs.
500 BCE	Hemp is introduced into northern Europe by the Scythians. An urn containing leaves and seeds of the cannabis plant, unearthed near Berlin, is dated to about this time.
500–100 BCE	Hemp spreads throughout northern Europe.
430 BCE	Herodotus reports on both ritual and recreational use of cannabis by the Scythians.

100–0 BCE	The psychotropic properties of cannabis are mentioned in a Chinese herbal titled *Pen Ts'ao Ching*, which is the written version of wisdom attributed to an emperor from about 2700 BCE.
70 CE	Dioscorides mentions the use of cannabis as a Roman medicine.
170	Galen (Roman) alludes to the psychoactivity of cannabis seed confections.
500–600	The Jewish Talmud mentions the euphoria-generating properties of cannabis.
900–1000	Scholars debate the pros and cons of eating hashish. Use spreads throughout Arabia.
1090–1256	In Khorasan, Persia, Hasan ibn al-Sabbah, the Old Man of the Mountain, recruits followers to commit assassinations, and legends develop around their supposed use of hashish. These legends are some of the earliest written tales of the discovery of the inebriating powers of cannabis and the supposed use of hashish.
Early 12th century	Hashish smoking is very popular throughout the Middle East.
12th century	Cannabis is introduced into Egypt by mystic devotees coming from Syria.
1155–1221	Persian legend of the Sufi master Sheik Haidar's of Khorasan's personal discovery of cannabis and its subsequent spread to Iraq, Bahrain, Egypt, and Syria. occurs. It is one of the earliest written narratives of the use of cannabis as an inebriant.

13th century	The oldest monograph on hashish, *Zahr al-'arish fi tahrim al-hashish,* is written. Ibn al-Baytar of Spain provides a description of psychoactive cannabis. Arab traders bring cannabis to the Mozambique coast of Africa.
1271–1295	During Marco Polo's accounts of his journeys to Asia, he gives second-hand reports of the story of Hasan ibn al-Sabbah and his "assassins" using hashish; this is the first time reports of cannabis coming to the attention of Europeans.
1378	Ottoman Emir Soudoun Scheikhouni issues one of the first edicts against the eating of hashish.
1549	Angolan slaves bring cannabis with them to the sugar plantations of northeastern Brazil. They were permitted to plant their cannabis between rows of cane and to smoke it between harvests.
17th century	Use of hashish, alcohol, and opium spreads among the population of occupied Constantinople.
1606–1632	The French and British cultivate cannabis for hemp at their colonies in Port Royal (1606), Virginia (1611), and Plymouth (1632).
Late 17th century	Hashish becomes a major trade item between Central Asia and South Asia.
1798	Napoleon discovers that much of the Egyptian lower class habitually uses hashish and declares a total prohibition. Nevertheless, soldiers returning to France bring the tradition with them.

1840	In America, medicinal preparations with a cannabis base are available. Hashish is available in Persian pharmacies.
1843	Le Club des Hachichins, or Hashish Eater's Club, is established in Paris.
1890	The Greek Department of Interior prohibits importation, cultivation, and use of hashish.
1890	Hashish is made illegal in Turkey.
1893–1894	Between 70,000 and 80,000 killograms of hashish are legally imported into India from Central Asia each year.
1906	The Pure Food and Drug Act is passed in the United States, regulating the labeling of products containing alcohol, opiates, cocaine, and cannabis, among others.
Early 20th century	Hashish smoking is very popular throughout the Middle East.
1915–1927	The nonmedical use of cannabis begins to be prohibited in the United States: California (1915), Texas (1919), Louisiana (1924), and New York (1927).
1926	Lebanese hashish production peaks after World War I until prohibited in 1926.
1928	Recreational use of cannabis is banned in Britain.
1920s–1930s	High-quality hashish is produced in Turkey near the Greek border.
1930s	Legally taxed imports of hashish continue into India from Central Asia.

1934–1935	The Chinese government moves to end all cannabis.
1936	Propaganda film *Reefer Madness* is made to scare American youth away from using cannabis.
1937	The federal Marihuana Tax Act makes cannabis illegal in the United States.
1945	Legal hashish consumption continues in India
1967	"Smash," the first hashish oil appears. Red Lebanese reaches California.
1970–1973	Huge fields of cannabis are cultivated for hashish production in Afghanistan.
1972	The Nixon-appointed Shafer Commission urges use of cannabis be re-legalized, but the recommendation is ignored. Medical research continues.
1973	The Afghan government makes hashish production and sales illegal.
1975	The FDA establishes the Compassionate Use program for medical marijuana.

1980s	Morocco becomes one of, if not the largest, hashish-producing and -exporting nations.
1988	After comprehensive hearings, DEA administrative law judge Francis Young finds that marijuana has clearly established medical use and should be reclassified as a prescriptive drug. His recommendation is ignored.
1993	Cannabis eradication efforts are conducted in Morocco.
1995	Introduction of hashish-making equipment and locally produced hashish appear in Amsterdam coffee shops.
2001	Britain's home secretary, David Blunkett, proposes relaxing the classification of cannabis from a Class B to Class C drug.
2003	Canada is first country in the world to offer medical marijuana to patients.
2006	Statistics indicate that marijuana is the most popular drug for American teens.
2010	California voters reject a proposition to legalize recreational marijuana.

3 Who Uses Marijuana?

What kind of person becomes an addict? Someone popular, with a lot of friends? Or someone who is different from everybody else, an outsider from the popular crowd, with only a few friends or none at all?

Anybody can become addicted to marijuana. It's not a "cool kid" thing, nor is it a "weird kid" thing either. Marijuana is available to almost all teens, and they choose to use it for a variety of reasons. A lot of these teens have told their stories on the Marijuana Anonymous Web site. Here's one of their stories:

> I used to be a guy who was always in the popular crowd. Right before high school began, I started being shunned by most of my friends. I had never lived with the fear that I had no friends, so I did almost anything to keep the two good friends I still had. One of the things I did was try pot for the first time. This was a big change from the way I lived when I was younger. I was an athlete, and

the last thing I thought I would get into was drugs. Drugs prevented me from being the best athlete I could be.

I entered high school, where smoking pot was "cool." I continued to smoke pot because that was what my new "cool" friends were into. The next three years were filled with many highs and lows, and everything seemed so superficial, including my friendships. This made me sad and depressed. I believe this was my "rock bottom."

I realized I could not live this way. There was one problem: I could not stop the routine of using drugs. It took being arrested twice, losing my license for two years, and my lawyer suggesting 12 Step meetings before I walked into Marijuana Anonymous.

Since then, my attitude and actions have changed and so has my direction in life. I do see a future in water polo. Luckily, I haven't killed my chance in athletics. Hopefully, I haven't killed all those relationships I damaged while I was using drugs. Either way, I know that my first priority is staying sober and keeping a clean head.

Marijuana is one of the most commonly used illicit drugs in the United States; more than 40 percent of people over the age of twelve have tried the drug at least once. In 2009, cannabis was involved in more than 376,000 emergency room visits, according to a study done by the Drug Abuse Warning Network (DAWN). This made it the second most prevalent abused drug. The majority (two-thirds) of these patients were male, and use was highest between the ages eighteen and twenty-four.

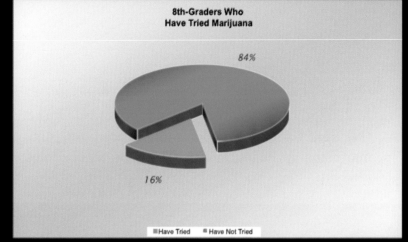

**8th-Graders Who
Have Tried Marijuana**

84%

16%

▪Have Tried   ▪ Have Not Tried

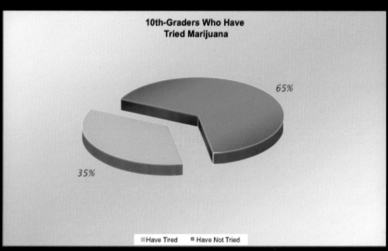

**10th-Graders Who Have
Tried Marijuana**

65%

35%

▪Have Tired   ▪ Have Not Tried

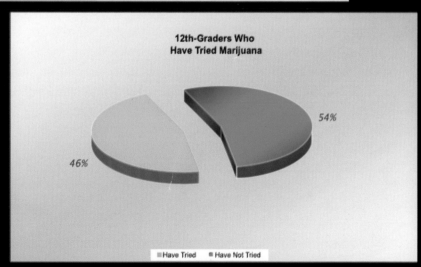

**12th-Graders Who
Have Tried Marijuana**

54%

46%

▪Have Tried   ▪ Have Not Tried

Pot: A Teenager's Drug?

In 2007, the National Household Survey on Drug Abuse (NHSDA) found that 1.7 million teenagers had used marijuana in the last month. The majority of adolescents

What Are the Risks?

Marijuana may be riskier than you think. It can limit your achievement in the classroom, on standardized tests, and in the future.

- Marijuana can hinder your ability to learn. Heavy marijuana use impairs young people's ability to concentrate and retain information.
- Marijuana use is linked to poorer grades. A teen with a "D" average is four times more likely to have used marijuana than a teen with an "A" average.
- Marijuana and underage drinking are linked to higher dropout rates. Students who drink or use drugs frequently are up to five times more likely than their peers to drop out of high school. A teenage marijuana user's odds of dropping out are more than twice that of a non-user.
- Research also shows that marijuana use is three times more likely to lead to dependence among adolescents than among adults. Research indicates that the earlier kids start using marijuana, the more likely they are to become dependent on this or other illicit drugs later in life.
- Teens who begin marijuana use at an early age when the brain is still developing may be more vulnerable to neuropsychological deficits, especially verbal abilities.
- Teens who are regular marijuana users often have short attention spans, decreased energy and ambition, poor judgment, impaired communications skills and diminished effectiveness in social situations.

(Source: National Youth Anti-Drug Media Campaign)

Marijuana Use in Past Year Among Persons Aged 12 or Older

- Total
- Male
- Female

know how to buy pot, or even know someone at school who deals drugs.

Throughout the 1990s, the use of marijuana among teenagers, especially those in middle school, increased. In 2006, 15.7 percent of eighth-graders were found to have used pot at least once, while 6 percent were regular users. This number rose as the ages increased, with 35 percent of tenth-graders having tried marijuana and 14.2 percent

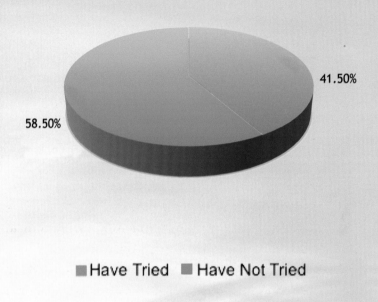

Percentage of People Age 12 & Over Who Have Tried Marijuana

41.50%

58.50%

■ Have Tried   ■ Have Not Tried

being regular users. By the time adolescents reach their senior year in high school, 42.3 percent will have tried pot at least once, while 18 percent will use it regularly.

Part of this increase in usage as teens' get older is because the perceived risk diminishes as getting the drug becomes easier. The 2009 National Survey of Drug Use and Health (NSDUH) reports that 40 percent of 8th-graders, 69 percent of 10th-graders, and 81 percent of 12th-graders think that marijuana would be fairly or very easy to purchase. The older teens have a greater exposure to marijuana, as well as other drugs, meaning that they are more likely to buy them because the perceived risk is smaller. Younger teens, who either don't know how to get drugs or think that it is more risky, are less likely to take the chance of purchasing pot.

However, teens are not the only group who uses marijuana. A 2002 study tested arrestees for various drugs, including marijuana. While they found that teens who have been arrested were more likely to have marijuana in their system (57 percent of males and 32 percent of females), adults arrested for various crimes often had consumed the drug as well, with 41 percent of males and 27 percent of females having marijuana in their system at the time of arrest.

According to the 2009 NSDUH more than 102 million Americans have tried marijuana at least once in their lives. Many of these (26 million) have used the drug in the past year. This was a significant increase from 1985, when 56.5 million people were found to have tried pot, 26.1 million of whom had used it in the last year. However, the percentage of people who had used it regularly went down; while 6 percent of people had used marijuana regularly in the 2009 study, more than 13.5 percent said the same in 1985.

Why Use Marijuana?

People start smoking pot for many reasons. Teens often try marijuana because of peer pressure; perhaps they see their friends or siblings use the drug and want to look

Marijuana Sellers, by Age Group (2002)

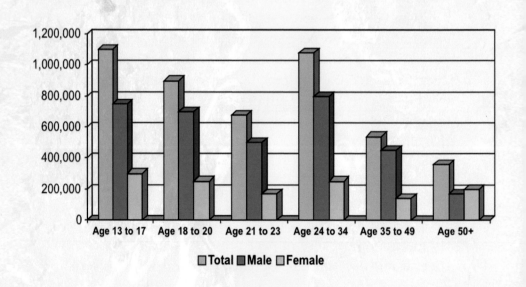

cool. However, marijuana is also used as an escape from problems at home and in school.

One reason teens specifically try marijuana is curiosity; many adolescents are attempting to try everything they can about the world. Pot also serves as a way to rebel against their parents; by using drugs, they can prove their independence to the world. Marijuana is a reminder of how they can make their own decisions and take care of themselves. Marijuana and other drugs can also serve as a release from problems. Whether it is a troubled home environment, an unfulfilling job, or social problems at school, life's problems make people more likely to turn to drugs or alcohol. Some people use cannabis to escape from their own inner demons; stress about school or work, depression, or any feelings of failure or helplessness can often cause depression. People searching for a release from these feelings may think the solution lies in marijuana.

Cannabis, along with other drugs, is seen as a way to relax and have fun. Many people use this drug at parties or when they're hanging out with their friends. They see it as a way to feel good and to reach a high. Because the drug is so popular, some users believe it is harmless; it's just another way to have a good time. However, marijuana, like any other illicit drug, can cause serious health and mental problems.

What Are the Dangers of Marijuana?

Another teen tells his story on the Marijuana Anonymous website:

> The first time I smoked weed was during the summer before eighth grade. I was really curious to see what it was all about. I had a few hits, but didn't really get stoned. Later, I smoked some more. I got so high I didn't even know what was going on. The next chance I got to get high, I jumped on it. The more I did it, the more I liked it. I loved the way pot played with my head.
>
> Finally, I got caught. I was grounded for a while, but I went right back to it. That happened over and over until my parents decided to put me in a chemical dependency program. I managed to still smoke pot on the day furthest from my drug tests. I tried all those purification concoctions, but my dad eventually found out. I was still determined not to let anybody rob me of my "God-given rights," so I continued to smoke bud and got "dirty" drug tests.

Some marijuana users might be surprised when they experience paranoia instead of an enjoyable high. Paranoia is just one of marijuana's possible side effects.

44 Chapter 4—What Are the Dangers of Marijuana?

My grades weren't really suffering so I saw no reason to stop. I kept getting into more trouble.

Finally, disaster struck. I was caught at school. My hearing to determine whether I am expelled or not happens very soon. My eyes have been opened. Getting caught once can ruin your life. By staying sober, I am getting all my privileges back. As for school, I hope to be allowed back in. My only job is to stay out of trouble.

The way that a person feels or reacts after taking marijuana can be decided by many factors. Not all people will have noticeable adverse effects, nor will everyone be able to escape with only a pleasant high. How a user reacts to cannabis can be affected by how many times a person has previously used the same drug, how much THC is present in the marijuana, how the drug is consumed, and whether or not the marijuana is mixed with other drugs or alcohol. Things like the user's expectations and where the drug is used can change how a person reacts as well.

There are many possible responses to a drug like marijuana. Some people may feel nothing at all after taking the drug. Others will feel a high—relaxed and happy. At other times, the marijuana results in physical feelings of hunger or thirst, often known as the "munchies." However, there are more adverse effects as well. Anxiety attacks and *paranoia* often accompany marijuana use, especially when it contains a lot of THC. One thing is sure, sooner or later all marijuana users suffer from some kind of unwanted side effect after using the drug. While some of these are short term and will go away after the THC is out of the person's system, some are more long term and can cause permanent damage to a user's body.

There is no such thing as a safe drug. Judgment, perception, and the future can become foggy.

46 Chapter 4—What Are the Dangers of Marijuana?

Marijuana can cause disruptions in perception, memory, and judgment. While these go away in time, especially when they occur in first-time users, they can last for at least six weeks after the drug is used. These cannabis-caused mental disorders are accepted as real diseases and have their own category in the *Diagnostic and Statistical Manual of Mental Disorders*, which is published by the American Psychiatric Association. These impairments include "cannabis intoxication," which is characterized by a loss of motor coordination, anxiety, a loss of judgment, withdrawal, and sometimes hallucinations. "Cannabis intoxication delirium" is another disorder; this one consists of a loss of memory and disorientation.

Bloodshot eyes are just one sign of possible marijuana use.

There are short-term physical effects to marijuana as well, including a raised heartbeat, bloodshot eyes, and/or dry mouth. These effects, as well as other, mental results of using the drug, can be magnified if any other drug is used at the same time. While all these side effects may sound bad enough, other more serious long-term consequences can occur as well.

Disruption of the Immune System

Smoking marijuana daily can lead to many adverse outcomes, especially where the immune system is concerned. Cells in the bronchial passages protect the body against any bacteria or other microorganisms that may be inhaled. Marijuana kills these cells, meaning that germs are more likely to get into a person's body and cause damage. Cannabis also reduces the body's ability to fight off harmful diseases. This means that people are more likely to die from an otherwise treatable disease, like pneumonia, which often proves fatal in people with weakened immune systems.

Marijuana kills helpful cells like macrophages and T-cells, which are responsible for fighting off germs in the body. When these are gone, diseases can overcome a person easily. Studies have shown that marijuana use may cause HIV patients to develop AIDS. The body is not only unable to fight against diseases like AIDS or cancer, but it is more susceptible to these and other diseases. While marijuana does not cause death in these cases, fatality is a very possible result; when people's immune systems are weakened by the drug, many diseases that would be easily fought off by a normal person can prove dangerous.

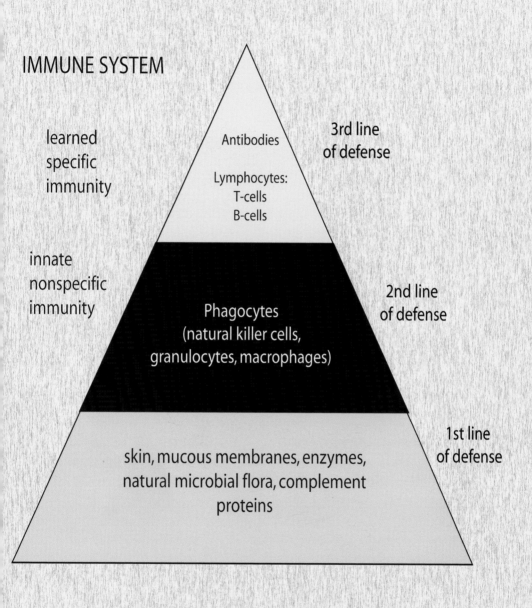

The human body's immune system protects it from disease. Drug use can weaken defense mechanisms, making it difficult for the body to fight off illness.

Respiratory Effects

A study that compared 173 people with cancer to 176 healthy people showed that smoking marijuana increases the chance of getting cancer in the head or neck. The more marijuana that was smoked, the higher the likelihood was.

Common Misconceptions About Marijuana

"Marijuana is harmless."
Smoking marijuana is every bit as bad as smoking cigarettes.

"It's not addictive."
More kids enter drug treatment for marijuana than for all other illicit drugs combined.

"It can't cause any real problems in the long term."
If you're smoking marijuana, you could do things that jeopardize your future, like having sex or getting in trouble with the law.

"Marijuana just makes you mellow."
Not always. Marijuana use is associated with violent behavior. Kids who use marijuana weekly are four times more likely to engage in violent behavior than those who don't.

"Marijuana's not as popular with teens as new drugs like ecstasy."
More kids use marijuana than cocaine, heroin, ecstasy and all other illicit drugs combined. Sixty percent of kids who use illicit drugs use marijuana only.

"If I smoke marijuana, I'm not hurting anyone else."
Marijuana trafficking is a big, often violent business, at home and abroad, that can lead to other crimes, including murder. When you buy marijuana, you're supporting that business.

(Source: Partnership for a Drug-Free America)

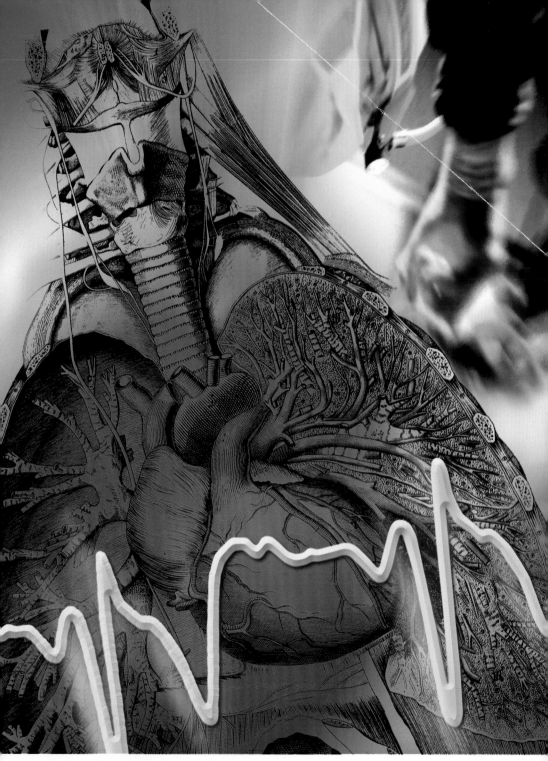

When one thinks of heart and lung diseases, it is usually in relation to tobacco. However, marijuana use can cause them as well.

Marijuana smoke contains many of the same carcinogens as are found in tobacco smoke.

Cancer isn't the only illness that can result from marijuana use. Emphysema and chronic bronchitis can lead to a need for supplemental oxygen.

When most people think of lung cancer, they think of cigarette smoke. However, marijuana can cause the same results, since both kinds of smoke contain many of the same toxic chemicals, including those known to cause cancer. Marijuana may even be more of a cancer threat than tobacco, since it contains four times the amount of tar that one regular cigarette does. The marijuana smoke also contains 50 to 75 percent more than tobacco smoke of the hydrocarbons that are proven to be **carcinogenic**. An enzyme that is present in marijuana smoke, which converts hydrocarbons to forms that can cause cancer, increases this effect. When you add this to the fact that people smoking a joint are more likely to hold the smoke in longer and breath it in deeper than tobacco users are, marijuana users are putting themselves at an even greater risk of developing cancer than tobacco users are.

Lung cancer is not the only adverse effect from marijuana on the respiratory system. Diseases like **emphysema**, *chronic* bronchitis, and respiratory tract infections also happen as a result of the inhalation of marijuana smoke. The toxins in the drug cause the air passages in the lungs to close up so they don't work as well, and the lungs to become inflamed.

A study of a group of 450 people found that those who use marijuana frequently have more health problems, especially involving their respiratory tract. These individuals felt sick more and missed more days of work than those who didn't smoke. This is not surprising when one considers that even occasional users frequently have burning and stinging in their mouths, as well as heavy coughs.

Adverse Effects of Marijuana on the Heart

Studies have shown that the chance of a heart attack goes up by more than four times in the first hour after someone smokes marijuana. While scientists are not sure why this occurs, they think it may be because marijuana use increases blood pressure and heart rate. It also causes the blood to lose some of its ability to carry oxygen, making the heart work harder. All these factors lead to the ideal conditions for a heart attack.

A Decrease in Mental Health

While marijuana can cause many problems to various body organs, the brain is also adversely affected. Studies have indicated a connection between marijuana and mental disorders like panic attacks, *flashbacks*, delusions, paranoia, and hallucinations. Marijuana has also been known to cause flare-ups in people who already have mental illnesses like *bipolar disorder* and *schizophrenia*.

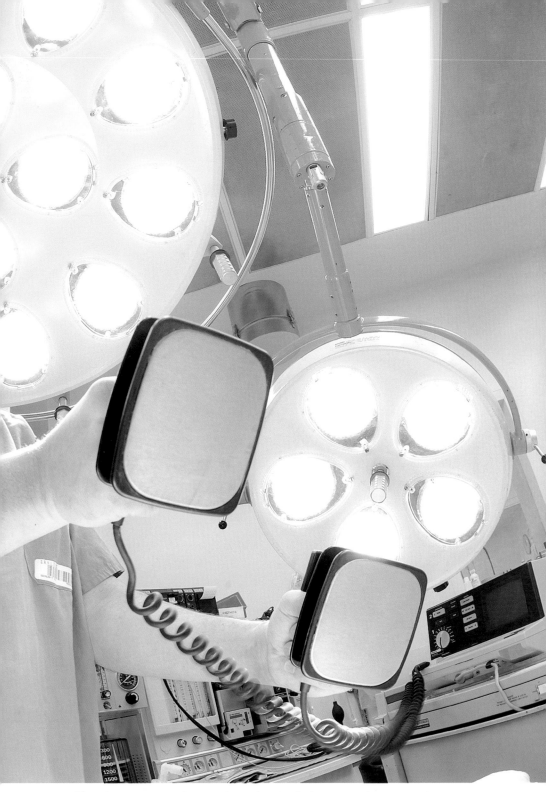

Though scientists aren't sure why, one's risk of a heart attack increases during the first hour after smoking a joint.

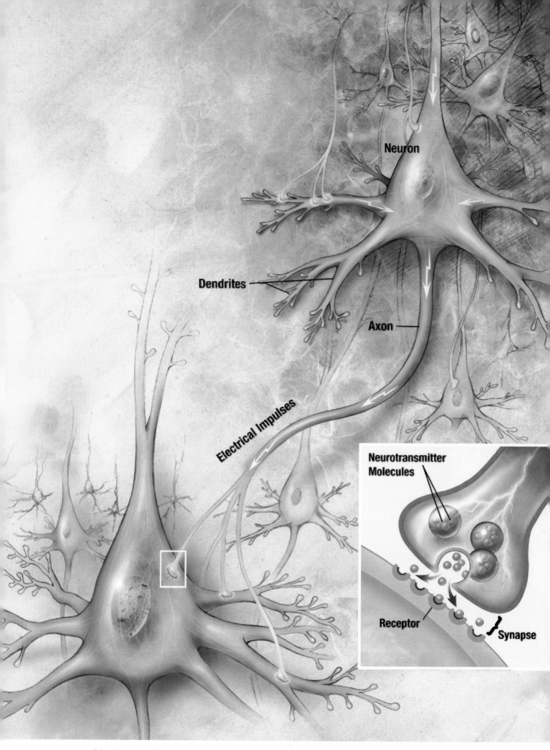

Neuron

Dendrites

Axon

Electrical Impulses

Neurotransmitter Molecules

Receptor

Synapse

Marijuana affects the brain's complex communication system, consisting of neurons and neurotransmitters. Emotions and thought processes are the two areas most affected.

Even first-time users can suffer from these results. Between 10 and 15 percent of people who smoked marijuana said that they felt confused or paranoid after using the drug and cited these as disadvantages of using cannabis. Twenty-seven percent said these feelings occurred regularly. This is caused by the binding of THC to the various brain cells (see chapter 1), many located in the areas of the brain that control memory, thought, and concentration.

Another result of long-term marijuana use is a change in the nerve cells that contain and produce dopamine. Dopamine regulates the feelings of motivation and the rewards we give ourselves for various behaviors. Marijuana is just one of many drugs that affects this chemical.

Because of the depression and anxiety that results from marijuana use, the drug can cause disruptions in daily life. People who use marijuana regularly are more likely to have trouble learning new skills or remembering information, making them fall behind in work or their everyday responsibilities. The good news is that these memory losses may not be permanent. Researchers recently tested a group of heavy marijuana smokers on their ability to remember words from a list. They were impaired while using the drug and for a week after quitting, but after about four weeks, their memories returned to normal.

Students have an especially hard time coping with marijuana use. Teens who use pot are less likely to graduate; they get lower grades in class and on standardized tests. While two people may score equally well on tests in fourth grade, by the time both are seniors, the marijuana smoker will score significantly lower.

Effects on the Reproduction System

Like many drugs, marijuana can lead to problems with the reproduction system. Both men and women have reported a temporary loss of fertility after using marijuana. The drug also has adverse effects on unborn babies. Some research has indicated that the use of marijuana during pregnancy can lead to miscarriages. Babies who are born to mothers who are marijuana users are often born prematurely or with low birth weights.

Children born to mothers who were frequent marijuana users were shown to be more nervous and apt to cry, as well as having a different response to visual stimuli than most infants that age. While this doesn't prove anything on its own, it may point to *neurological* defects. This conclusion is reinforced by the fact that between the ages of infancy and preschool, these children are more likely to have behavioral issues and a poorer performance in school as they continue to grow.

Driving Under the Influence—
It's Not Just About Alcohol

As already stated, marijuana influences skills like coordination, the ability to concentrate, and reaction time. While this is never good, it can be especially dangerous when a person is driving. People under the influence of cannabis, as with other drugs or alcohol, have a hard time responding to signals on the road in time to avoid an accident. These necessary skills are impaired for at least four to six hours after using one joint, long after the user has lost the euphoria of a high.

Studies of patients in shock-trauma units because of car accidents have shown that about 15 percent of

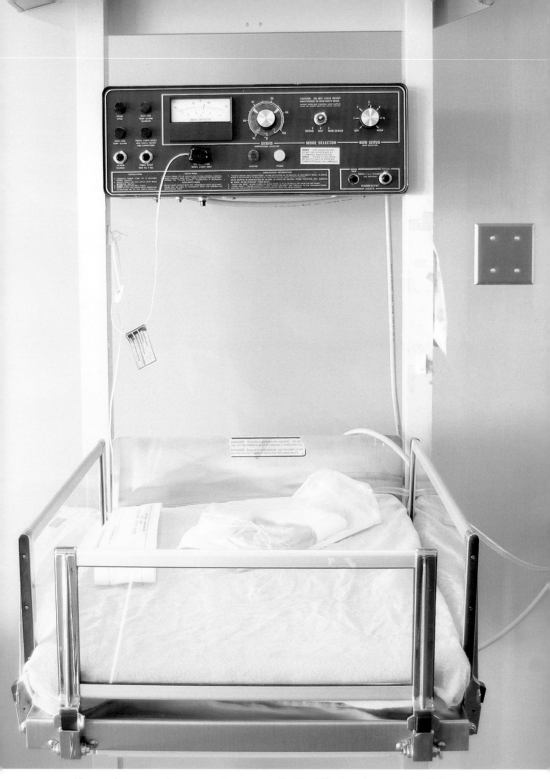

Men and women who use marijuana may find it difficult to have a baby. If they do get pregnant, there can be complications, including the risk of giving birth prematurely.

The "I" in DUI stands for more than alcohol. You can be charged with driving under the influence if you've been using drugs such as marijuana.

those who had been driving a car or motorcycle when they crashed had been under the influence of marijuana. When reckless drivers were tested at the scene for drugs, more than 33 percent tested positive for marijuana; 12 percent were positive for both pot and cocaine.

Marijuana: An Addictive Drug

Long-term marijuana use often leads to addiction. People start craving the drug—they are unable to function without it. More than 150,000 people each year get treatment for their marijuana addictions, which are characterized by an uncontrollable urge for the drug. Cannabis addicts use the drug even when they know that the drug is not in their best interests. Symptoms of marijuana addiction include:

- a tolerance for the drug
- the inability to cut down or control marijuana use
- the use of a huge amount of time to smoke marijuana
- a decrease in social activities because of marijuana use
- continued use, even though it is causing the individual problems

Cannabis can be both physically and emotionally addictive. Abusers define themselves by the drug. They are always thinking about it and when they will next get high. They think of marijuana as a miracle cure for all their problems.

When these people do try to quit, they often find that they can't. They may experience irritability, insomnia,

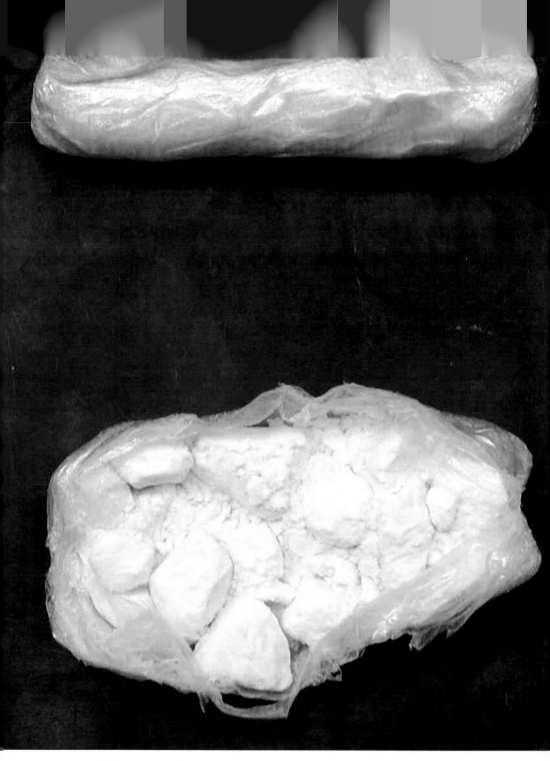

Will someone who uses marijuana go on to use harder drugs? Though no one knows for sure, most who use harder drugs, such as cocaine, report they started with marijuana.

62 Chapter 4—What Are the Dangers of Marijuana?

and anxiety when they attempt to stop using marijuana. These are all signs of withdrawal; the body is now dependent on the drug and finds it hard to survive without it. Withdrawal is also characterized by tension and decreases in appetite. While symptoms appear within twenty-four hours of the last dose of cannabis, they can last up to twenty-eight days.

Other Effects

Marijuana stays in the body long after the drug is consumed. The body, especially the fat, absorbs THC, and it is transformed into **metabolites** in an attempt for the body to rid itself of the foreign substance. These metabolites can be present in urine tests for up to a week after use.

Another problem is that marijuana is often considered a gateway drug, a drug that leads to other, heavier drugs. While this is not technically proven, it has been shown that very few adolescents use other illicit drugs without trying marijuana first. Part of this is because marijuana is relatively easy to obtain, and use puts people in contact with people who can buy and sell other drugs as well. After teens learn how to buy marijuana, they can also easily get hold of other substances.

Clearly, marijuana use has serious consequences. Physical and mental side effects are only one side of the story. Marijuana use has legal and social ramifications as well.

5 What Are the Legal Consequences of Using Marijuana?

Almost everyone knows that marijuana is illegal. But what does this mean exactly? Each state has its own laws about the consequences of possessing and dealing marijuana. There are different kinds of laws, all of which attempt to monitor the use of cannabis. However, while each state has individual laws, they all must conform to federal regulations.

Federal Marijuana Policies

Federal law states that possessing marijuana for the first time is a **misdemeanor**. The punishment is up to one year in prison and/or a $1,000 fine. This goes up slightly for a second offense, when the law states that an offender must spend a minimum of fifteen days in prison and pay a $2,500 fine. However, after this the consequences rise. After the second offense, anyone caught possessing marijuana faces anywhere from three months to three years in prison as well as a $5,000 fine.

The laws are even harsher for dealing marijuana. While possession is only a misdemeanor, selling cannabis is a felony. Someone caught dealing faces anywhere from five years to life in prison, depending on how many times he has been caught, as well as a fine that may vary from $250,000 for small quantities of the drug to $4,000,000. These penalties double if one is caught dealing marijuana to a minor (someone under the age of twenty-one) or when within a hundred feet of a school.

Life in prison is not the worst thing these drug dealers may face; the death penalty is considered an acceptable punishment in some situations. If the defendant is the leader of a continuing enterprise to deal drugs and if the quantity of marijuana exceeds 60,000 kilograms, then the dealer can be sentenced to death.

While the federal government implements all of the above policies, each state legislature has introduced its own marijuana laws as well. These laws can be broken up into different types—tax stamps, DUID laws, industrial hemp laws, medical use, mandatory minimum sentences, decriminalization, and conditional release laws.

Tax Stamp Laws

Tax stamp laws require possessors of drugs to buy stamps and attach them to the drugs. These stamps are issued by

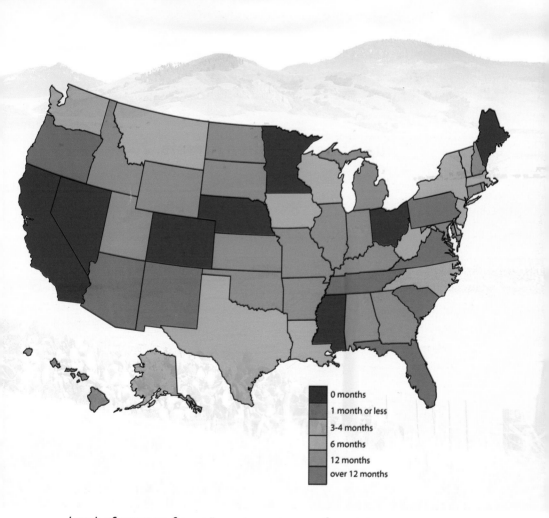

	0 months
	1 month or less
	3-4 months
	6 months
	12 months
	over 12 months

Length of sentences for marijuana possession vary from state to state across the United States.

Drug Abuse Violation Arrests, 2009

6%

48%

46%

■ All other drugs ■ Marijuana Possession ■ Marijuana Sale/Manufacture

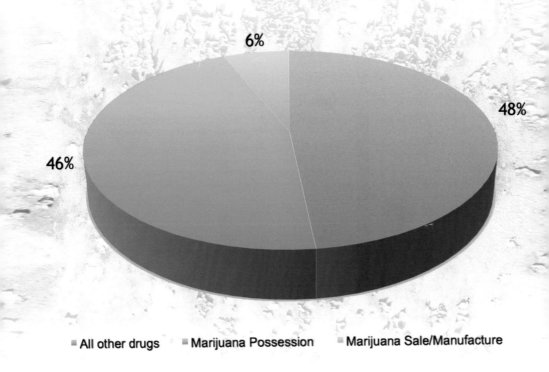

the state and are priced depending on the amount of the drug that is possessed; most states price these stamps at about $3.50 per gram of marijuana. Twenty states have these laws in place, including Texas, Kansas, California, Alabama, Tennessee, Kentucky, and Indiana.

While these laws are in place in many states, few people follow them. Understandably, drug users fear that buying stamps will lead the police to arrest them for possession. Others are unaware that these laws exist at all. If someone is arrested for drug possession and then found to have broken these laws, the penalty will vary according to each state. Some states, like Georgia, deal with this infraction through a relatively lenient misdemeanor penalty. Other states, like Minnesota, have harsher punishments; in some cases, defendants may face up to seven years in jail, as well as a fine of up to $14,000. This is in addition to whatever the punishment was for possession. The average penalty involves paying up to 200 percent of what the tax would have been as a fine and a prison sentence of up to five years.

DUID

DUID stands for "driving under the influence of drugs." In general, this means that drivers must not have any controlled substance in their blood, but there are many subcategories of DUID laws, all with varying punishments. All states have some type of DUID law.

Effect-based DUID laws are the most common type. In these laws, prosecutors must prove to a court that a driver's impairment was caused by the ingestion of an illegal substance like marijuana. This proof is mostly based on drug tests or any evidence gathered at the scene (like the results of a sobriety test or proof of reckless or impaired driving). The punishment is based on laws that forbid drivers to operate a motor vehicle while under the influence or when they are incapable of driving safely because of drug use.

Per se DUID laws punish drivers who have higher than a certain level of a drug present in their systems. For example, in most states, drunk driving laws state that drivers are drunk and therefore breaking the law if they have a blood alcohol content of more than 0.08 percent. These laws are uncommon for illicit substances like marijuana, however. This is because scientists and lawmakers are unable to agree about a specific level at which impairment is certain. This lack of *consensus* makes it difficult to both implement laws and convict drivers.

One response to this inability to agree on a level is to establish zero tolerance per se laws. Basically, these laws state that drivers must not have any detectable level of an illicit drug present in their systems while operating a motor vehicle. The penalty for this is most often a mandatory twenty-four-hour imprisonment as well as up to twelve months in prison. Nineteen states have implemented this type of policy, including Alaska, Arizona, Delaware, Georgia, Illinois Indiana, Iowa, Michigan, Minnesota, Mississippi, Nevada, North Carolina, Ohio, Pennsylvania, Rhode Island, South Carolina, Utah, Virginia, and Wisconsin. Many people are against these zero tolerance laws; they argue that many drivers are sober, even if they do show minute traces of a drug in their system. This is especially an issue in the case of marijuana, where THC may be found in the blood for days after use.

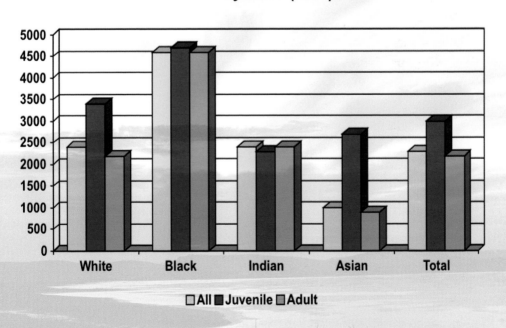

Marijuana Possession Arrest Rate per 100,000 Users, by Race (2002)

Marijuana has been used for medicinal purposes for many years, often as an adjunct to other medications prescribed for cancer patients.

Industrial Hemp Laws

Nine states currently allow the growing of industrial hemp—a plant similar to that from which marijuana is produced. However, a bill was recently introduced into Congress that would allow for industrial hemp farming. Hemp is used to make such goods as paper, paint, clothing, plastics, food, insulation, and animal feed. It is often considered a desirable crop, since it has a much higher yield than crops like cotton. It also requires fewer pesticides and can be grown more than once a season, since the growing cycle is only a hundred days. Hemp seeds are also used as a food; they contain protein and a high amount of amino acids that humans need to survive.

In the United States alone, 1.9 million pounds of hemp are imported annually, as well as 450,000 pounds of the hemp seeds and 331 pounds of hempseed oil. While federal law bans many hemp products, hemp fibers, sterile seeds, and foodstuffs that contain no THC are allowed into the country.

During the 1920s, hemp was used in Canada as the base in oils and varnishes, clothing, ropes, sails, seed food and oil, paper, and as a medicinal remedy. In 1928, the growing of hemp was outlawed in an anti-marijuana movement. Many Canadians, including hemp farmers, had not heard the word "marijuana" at that time. It came as a surprise to many farmers that laws concerning a drug meant that they could no longer grow their hemp crops.

Except for brief periods during wartime, growing hemp was prohibited until 1988. In May of that year, the law was changed to allow a "test period" during which the commercial growing of hemp was allowed. Farmers wanting to grow commercial hemp today are required to obtain a government permit.

Medical Marijuana

Marijuana is used for many medical uses; it can reduce nausea and vomiting, promote weight gain by increasing the appetite, and decrease the pressure in the inner eye caused by *glaucoma*. It can also be used to reduce illnesses like migraine headaches, depression, insomnia, and various chronic pains. Because of this, eighteen states and counting have made marijuana legal for medical use, with a doctor's prescription, or are considering such laws. These states include Vermont, Maryland, Rhode Island, Hawaii, Oregon, and California.

Mandatory Minimum Sentence

This law means just what the name implies—when someone is caught with illegal possession of marijuana, that person must be sentenced for at least a minimum time in prison. Most of the time, these prisoners are not eligible for parole until the minimum time is up. Many U.S. states have implemented this law in regard to marijuana possession.

Officially, the cultivation and possession of marijuana in Canada is illegal. However, the possession of small amounts of marijuana for personal use is widely tolerated. Under the Liberal government, Canadian lawmakers have attempted since 2002 to decriminalize the possession of small amounts of marijuana, while stiffening penalties for possessing large amounts of the drug. Bills to change existing marijuana laws were introduced to Parliament in 2003 and 2004, but were voted down and have not been re-introduced.

The courts continue to struggle with marijuana as a legal issue.

In some states, judges use alternative sentences for first-time offenders. With some programs, the incident doesn't even go on a permanent record.

76 Chapter 5—What Are the Legal Consequences of Using Marijuana?

Decriminalization of Marijuana

Since the year 1973, several states, including Alaska, New York, Maine, Mississippi, and Nebraska, have decriminalized marijuana to some extent. This means that there are reduced punishments for marijuana possession in small amounts. Jail time is rarely involved, and many states no longer put arrest for marijuana possession on a permanent criminal record. However, these laws do not apply when it is a second arrest, when more than small amounts of marijuana are in possession, or when a driver is convicted of DUID.

Conditional Release

The final type of marijuana law is conditional release. This is when the state allows a release, or probation, for a first-time user instead of prison time or a court trial. If the probation is successful, then the defendant will be released with a clean record. Twenty-four states have implemented this type of policy, including Oregon, Colorado, Kansas, Oklahoma, and Georgia.

All these laws are attempts to find a legal solution to a social and medical problem. Not everyone agrees that these laws are effective, let alone just. Others, however, feel that laws should be even more stringent. A lot of controversy surrounds marijuana.

Answers to Teen's Questions About Marijuana

1. Can smoking marijuana harm or even kill me?

Marijuana is not usually toxic enough to kill you, but if you mix this drug with other drugs or do something that requires brain skills and coordination (like driving a car), then yes, smoking pot can kill you. Marijuana affects nerve cells in the part of the brain where memories are formed, so someone who has smoked marijuana may have difficulty studying, remembering recent events, and handling complex tasks. This is why teenagers who get high and drive are involved in auto accidents.

2. What are the long-term effects of smoking marijuana?

Studies have shown that someone who smokes five joints may be taking in as many cancer-causing chemicals as someone who smokes a full pack of cigarettes. Also, heavy doses of marijuana may delay the onset of puberty in young men and disrupt the normal monthly menstrual cycle in young women.

3. Can smoking marijuana while pregnant harm an unborn baby?

Babies born to mothers who regularly smoke marijuana are usually shorter, weigh less and have smaller head sizes than those whose mothers do not use the drug. Smaller babies are more likely to develop health problems. Studies show children of mothers who smoked marijuana have more serious system problems than those whose mothers did not.

4. Does smoking marijuana lead to other drugs?

Very few people use other illegal drugs without first trying marijuana. Using marijuana puts you in contact with people who are users and sellers of other drugs. So by smoking marijuana, you will be exposed to more drugs and encouraged to try them. And once high on pot, you might be more willing to try something stronger.

5. Can I be forced to take a drug test that will tell people if I'm using marijuana?

It is your parents' job to protect you from things that can harm you, so only your parents can insist that you take a drug test. However, employers, coaches, and others may ask you to take a drug test as a condition of participation in an organization. They may even require you to take follow-up drug tests once you have joined them. You do not have to take these tests, but if you don't, you probably will not be allowed to stay in the organization. Still, it's your choice.

6. How does smoking marijuana increase the dangers from getting drunk?

Smoking marijuana suppresses your body's instinctual need to throw-up bad things in your stomach. If you have been smoking pot while binge drinking, your body will not be able to purge when your blood alcohol level reaches a dangerous level. That is why each year we read about kids dying at college drinking parties. Too often they were also smoking pot.

7. If I get caught using marijuana, can that hurt my chances of getting into college?

Getting into a good college is harder than ever these days. Most community colleges and universities will look beyond the grades and check all of your high school student records. A history of drug use, possession, buying, or selling drugs may kill your chances of getting into the college or university of your choice.

8. Can I get into trouble for holding marijuana for someone else?

Yes. It does not matter where you keep them (in your backpack, locker, bedroom, etc.), if you have ANY illegal drugs in your possession, the police will consider them yours. You can go to jail for this. Never accept drugs or a package "to hold" for someone else. If you do not know what is inside, do not take it. It is not worth the risk.

9. If I think a friend is using marijuana, should I tell his parents or a teacher?

A true friend doesn't stand by and watch a friend hurt himself. This is a hard decision to make—be sure to consider all the possible consequences your friend faces if you don't tell.

(Source: KidsGrowth.com)

Controversial Issues

Lots of North Americans believe that marijuana should be legalized. Others are just as convinced that marijuana use needs to remain illegal. There are voices on each side of the debate, with hundreds of arguments about why marijuana should or should not be legalized. One individual wrote her story on the website called Marijuana4Pain:

Hello, I'm Tiffany. I'm not going to bore you with the details of my medical history, just a brief explanation. I've had 2 back surgeries. First was to repair a ruptured disk and the second was a fusion at the same level. During the first surgery, the doctor cut my dura sack (lining surrounding the spine), which brought on a spinal disease called arachnoiditis, which produces quite a bit of pain in my lower back, butt, and legs. Arachnoiditis is basically scar tissue in the spine, which is "attached to" and "squeezing" the nerves in my spine. I was diagnosed back in '97 and have been through a big variety of medicines. My chief complaint has

Marijuana by the Acre!

The U.S. Census of 1850 counted 8,327 hemp "plantations" (minimum 2,000-acre farm) growing cannabis hemp.

been the side effects and how much the pills cost! Seeing my frustration, my mother suggested I try marijuana for the pain. I did and it's been a blessing for my husband and I. (He was affected by my moodiness and sadness, side effects from the pills.) I am more productive now than when I was taking pain pills. Every doctor that I go to knows that I use marijuana and have watched my progress. It is no longer an issue with them because there is a huge reduction in the amount of pills that I'm prescribed. It doesn't feel right that I am considered a criminal to most because of my choice of pain relief . . . even though it wasn't my first choice.

For most of human history, marijuana has been completely legal. It's not a recently discovered plant, nor is it a long-standing law. Marijuana has been illegal for less than 1 percent of the time that it's been in use. When your grandparents were born, it was probably legal.

America's first marijuana law was enacted at Jamestown Colony, Virginia, in 1619—but it wasn't a law *against* marijuana. Instead, it ordered all farmers to grow Indian hempseed. Several other "must-grow" laws were passed over the next two hundred years; for instance, you could be jailed for not growing hemp during times of shortage in Virginia between 1763 and 1767. During most of that time, hemp was also legal **tender;** you could even pay your taxes with hemp. Hemp was such a critical crop for a number of purposes that the government went out of its way to encourage its growth.

Early settlers to Jamestown Colony were ordered to grow hemp. Noncompliance could send colonists to jail.

The Mormons' headquarters in Salt Lake City; Mormons returned to Utah after a trip to Mexico, and they brought marijuana with them. The church disapproved, and Utah became the first state to outlaw its use.

84 Chapter 6—Controversial Issues

The Mexican Connection to Marijuana's Bad Name

In the early 1900s, the white people in America's western states weren't always happy about the influx of Mexican Americans. The revolution in Mexico in 1910 spilled over the border, with the American army clashing with Mexican bandit Pancho Villa. Later in that decade, bad feelings developed between the small farmers and the large farms that used cheaper Mexican labor. When the **Great Depression** began, tensions grew still greater as jobs and resources became scarce.

Many white people were quick to notice all the ways that Mexican Americans were "different"—and these differences were viewed as dangerous and suspicious. One of those "suspicious" differences had to do with marijuana: some Mexicans smoked marijuana and had brought the plant with them across the border.

However, the first state law outlawing marijuana did so not because of Mexicans using the drug. Oddly enough, it was because of Mormons using it. Mormons who traveled to Mexico in 1910 came back to Salt Lake City with marijuana. The Mormon Church was not pleased and ruled against use of the drug. Since the state of Utah automatically enshrined church doctrine into law, the first state marijuana prohibition was established in 1915.

Other states quickly followed suit with their own marijuana prohibition laws, including Wyoming (1915), Texas (1919), Iowa (1923), Nevada (1923), Oregon (1923), Washington (1923), Arkansas (1923), and Nebraska (1927). These laws tended to be specifically targeted against the Mexican American population. For example, when Montana outlawed marijuana in 1927, *The Butte Montana Standard* reported a legislator's comment: "When some beet field peon takes a few traces of this stuff

. . . he thinks he has just been elected president of Mexico, so he starts out to execute all his political enemies." In Texas, a senator said on the floor of the State Senate: "All Mexicans are crazy, and this stuff [marijuana] is what makes them crazy."

Jazz

Meanwhile, in the Eastern states, the presence of marijuana was blamed on both Latin Americans and black jazz musicians. Marijuana and jazz traveled from New Orleans to Chicago, and then to New York City's Harlem, where marijuana became a part of the music scene, even entering the language of the black hits of the time (Louis Armstrong's "Muggles," Cab Calloway's "That Funny Reefer Man," Fats Waller's "Viper's Drag"). Again, racism played a part in the charge made against marijuana; one Eastern newspaper in 1934 editorialized: "Marihuana influences Negroes to look at white people in the eye, step on white men's shadows and look at a white woman twice."

Fear Tactics

Rumors spread across America. One said that Mexicans, black Americans, and foreigners were luring white children into their clutches with marijuana; another rumor had to do with "assassins." Marco Polo brought some of the earliest stories of marijuana back to Europe, where he told of "hashish-eaters" or *hashashin*, from which the term "assassin" was derived. In the original stories, these professional killers were given large doses of hashish and brought to the ruler's garden (to give them a glimpse of

As jazz musicians moved north from New Orleans, so did marijuana. The association between music and drugs has continued for many years.

Marijuana—Mind-Altering Weed 87

Federal Bureau of Narcotics director Harry J. Anslinger took advantage of prejudice running rampant in 1930s' America. He claimed that most marijuana smokers were members of minority groups.

the paradise that awaited them on successful completion of their mission). Then, after the effects of the drug disappeared, the assassin would fulfill his ruler's wishes with cool, calculating loyalty. By the 1930s, however, the story had changed. Dr. A. E. Fossier wrote in the 1931 *New Orleans Medical and Surgical Journal*: "Under the influence of hashish those fanatics would madly rush at their enemies, and ruthlessly massacre every one within their grasp." Soon, marijuana was linked to violent behavior.

Federal Approaches to Drug Prohibition

In 1930, a new division in the Treasury Department was established—the Federal Bureau of Narcotics—and Harry J. Anslinger was named director. This marked the beginning of the U.S. government's war against marijuana.

Anslinger preyed on America's racism, prejudice, and fear to draw national attention to marijuana. The following statements made by Anslinger indicate his mindset:

"There are 100,000 total marijuana smokers in the U.S., and most are Negroes, Hispanics, Filipinos, and entertainers. Their Satanic music, jazz, and swing, result from marijuana use."

"The primary reason to outlaw marijuana is its effect on the degenerate races."

"Marijuana is an addictive drug which produces in its users insanity, criminality, and death."

"Reefer makes darkies think they're as good as white men."

Newspapers and other media spread stories telling the horrors of marijuana and other drugs. Hashish was claimed to cause bloodlust in its users.

"Marijuana leads to pacifism and communist brainwashing."

"You smoke a joint and you're likely to kill your brother."

"Marijuana is the most violence-causing drug in the history of mankind."

Meanwhile, **yellow journalism** was selling newspapers across America. Lurid news stories about the dangers of marijuana helped to further shape public opinion. Here are some samples:

MARIHUANA MAKES FIENDS OF BOYS IN THIRTY DAYS
HASHISH GOADS USERS TO BLOODLUST

By the tons it is coming into this country—the deadly, dreadful poison that racks and tears not only the body, but the very heart and soul of every human being who once becomes a slave to it in any of its cruel and devastating forms. . . . Marihuana is a short cut to the insane asylum. Smoke marihuana cigarettes for a month and what was once your brain will be nothing but a storehouse of horrid specters. Hasheesh makes a murderer who kills for the love of killing out of the mildest mannered man who ever laughed at the idea that any habit could ever get him.

Users of marijuana become STIMULATED as they inhale the drug and are LIKELY TO DO ANYTHING. Most crimes of violence in this section, especially in country districts, are laid to users of that drug.

Was it marijuana, the new Mexican drug, that nerved the murderous arm of Clara Phillips when she hammered out her victim's life in Los Angeles?

THREE-FOURTHS OF THE CRIMES of violence in this country today are committed by DOPE SLAVES—that is a matter of cold record.

The Marihuana Tax Act of 1937

In 1937, Anslinger went to Congress with a collection of evidence against marijuana. The only dissenting voice came from Dr. William C. Woodward from the American Medical Association (AMA). Dr. Woodward reproached Harry Anslinger and the Bureau of Narcotics for distorting earlier AMA statements that had nothing to do with marijuana and making them appear to be AMA endorsement for Anslinger's view. He also spoke out against the Bureau's use of the term marijuana, while not publicizing that the government was actually talking about cannabis or hemp. At this point, marijuana (or marihuana) was a *sensationalist* word that had not been connected in most people's minds to the existing cannabis/hemp plant. Thus, many who had legitimate reasons to oppose an anti-hemp bill weren't even aware that one was being considered.

Woodward went on to state that the AMA questioned the approach of the hearings, coming close to an

During congressional hearings, Anslinger based much of his testimony on the supposed position of the AMA. Though he misrepresented the organization's position, the Marihuana Tax Act of 1937 passed.

Marijuana—Mind-Altering Weed 93

outright accusation of misconduct by Anslinger and the committee:

> That there is a certain amount of narcotic addiction of an objectionable character no one will deny. The newspapers have called attention to it so prominently that there must be some grounds for [their] statements. It has surprised me, however, that the facts on which these statements have been based have not been brought before this committee by competent primary evidence. We are referred to newspaper publications concerning the prevalence of marihuana addiction. We are told that the use of marihuana causes crime.
>
> But yet no one has been produced from the Bureau of Prisons to show the number of prisoners who have been found addicted to the marihuana habit. An informed inquiry shows that the Bureau of Prisons has no evidence on that point.
>
> You have been told that school children are great users of marihuana cigarettes. No one has been summoned from the Children's Bureau to show the nature and extent of the habit, among children.
>
> Inquiry of the Children's Bureau shows that they have had no occasion to investigate it and know nothing particularly of it.
>
> Inquiry of the Office of Education—and they certainly should know something of the prevalence of the habit among the school children of the country, if there is a prevalent habit—indicates that they have had no occasion to investigate and know nothing of it.

Proponents of the Marihuana Tax Act claimed that large numbers of schoolchildren used marijuana. Clearly the claim was exaggerated.

People such as Harry Anslinger wanted to keep films such as Reefer Madness out of traditional theaters and the new drive-ins. It has become a cult classic and is available on DVD. A musical version was released in 2005.

Moreover, there is in the Treasury Department itself, the Public Health Service, with its Division of Mental Hygiene. The Division of Mental Hygiene was, in the first place, the Division of Narcotics. It was converted into the Division of Mental Hygiene, I think, about 1930. That particular Bureau has control at the present time of the narcotics farms that were created about 1929 or 1930 and came into operation a few years later. No one has been summoned from that Bureau to give evidence on that point.

Informal inquiry by me indicates that they have had no record of any marihuana of Cannabis addicts who have ever been committed to those farms.

The bureau of Public Health Service has also a division of pharmacology. If you desire evidence as to the pharmacology of Cannabis, that obviously is the place where you can get direct and primary evidence, rather than the indirect hearsay evidence.

The chairman of the hearing countered by reading an editorial from the *Washington Times*:

The marihuana cigarette is one of the most insidious of all forms of dope, largely because of the failure of the public to understand its fatal qualities.

The Nation is almost defenseless against it, having no Federal laws to cope with it and virtually no organized campaign for combating it.

The result is tragic.

School children are the prey of peddlers who infest school neighborhoods.

High school boys and girls buy the destructive weed without knowledge of its capacity of harm, and conscienceless dealers sell it with **impunity.**

This is a national problem, and it must have national attention.

The fatal marihuana cigarette must be recognized as a deadly drug, and American children must be protected against it.

On August 2, 1937, marijuana became illegal at the federal level. Most Americans agreed that this was a good first step in the war against marijuana. Others, however, were outraged.

Anslinger continued his own personal war against the drug. He banned the Canadian movie *Drug Addict*, a 1946 documentary that realistically depicted drug addicts and law enforcement efforts. He even tried to get Canada to ban the movie in their own country, or failing that, to prevent U.S. citizens from seeing the movie in Canada. Canada refused.

Legal Marijuana?

Marijuana can be dangerous. Some Americans, however, feel the dangers have been exaggerated. Others point to the fact that alcohol and tobacco are equally dangerous, and yet both are legal for adults to use. These Americans believe that the benefits of legalizing marijuana outweigh any risks that may occur from marijuana use.

Many of the people who want marijuana legalized think that the recreational use of marijuana should still be against the law, but that medical use should be allowed. For these individuals, ending people's pain is essential. They point out that marijuana's possible medical risks are no more dangerous than those of many other prescription

In 2002, former U.S. Surgeon General Joycelyn Elders spoke in favor of legalizing marijuana. She contends that the potential for a fatal overdose of marijuana is far less than of alcohol and other legal drugs.

Pros

Individuals who favor the legalization of marijuana cite these facts:

- The University of Mississippi has grown marijuana (including a placebo with virtually no THC) for the U.S. government since 1968. Each year the University of Mississippi grows 1.5 acres, 6.5 acres, or none, depending upon demand.

- In every vote or poll on medical marijuana chronicled since 1975, more than 50 percent of respondents were in favor of medical marijuana.

- According to the U.S. Drug Abuse Warning Network (DAWN) in 2000, marijuana alone has never caused an overdose death.

- In 1978, the U.S. government started the Compassionate Investigational New Drug (IND) program, upon a court order, to supply about 300 marijuana cigarettes per month to seriously ill patients approved for the program. The program was shut down in 1991, but a very few of those patients, as of 2012, continue to receive the free government marijuana.

- Marijuana extracts were the first-, second-, or third-most prescribed medicines in the United States each year from 1842 until the 1890s.

- The 1999 U.S. Institute of Medicine (IOM) report, commissioned by the U.S. government, recommended that under certain narrow conditions, marijuana should be medically available to some patients, even though "numerous studies suggest that marijuana smoke is an important risk factor in the development of respiratory disease."

(Source: http://www.medicalmarijuanaprocon.org/pop/curiosities.htm)

drugs, and they feel that consumers should be allowed to make the choice for themselves. As former U.S. Surgeon General Joycelyn Elders stated in 2002:

Tobacco, through its direct physical effects, kills many thousands of people every year. So does alcohol. And it is easy to fatally overdose on alcohol, just as you can fatally overdose on prescription drugs, or even over-the-counter drugs, such as aspirin or acetaminophen (the active ingredient in Tylenol). I don't believe that anyone has ever died from a marijuana overdose.

Cons

Americans against the legalization of marijuana cites these statistics:

• Marijuana contains more than 400 chemicals, including most of the harmful substances found in tobacco smoke. Smoking one marijuana cigarette deposits about four times more tar into the lungs than a filtered tobacco cigarette. The British Lung Foundation reports that 3–4 marijuana cigarettes a day are as dangerous to the lungs as twenty or more tobacco cigarettes a day. (Other experts disagree, however.)

• Harvard University researchers report the risk of a heart attack is five times higher than usual in the hour after smoking marijuana.

• The risk of using cocaine is estimated to be more than 104 times greater for those who have tried marijuana than for those who have never tried it.

• Smoking marijuana can injure or destroy lung tissue. In fact, marijuana smoke contains 50–70 percent more of some cancer-causing chemicals than does tobacco smoke.

• Reaction time for motor skills, such as driving, is reduced by 41 percent after smoking one joint and is reduced 63 percent after smoking two joints.

• There have been over 7,000 published scientific and medical studies documenting the damage that marijuana poses. Not one study has shown marijuana to be safe.

(Source: http://www.medicalmarijuanaprocon.org/pop/curiosities.htm)

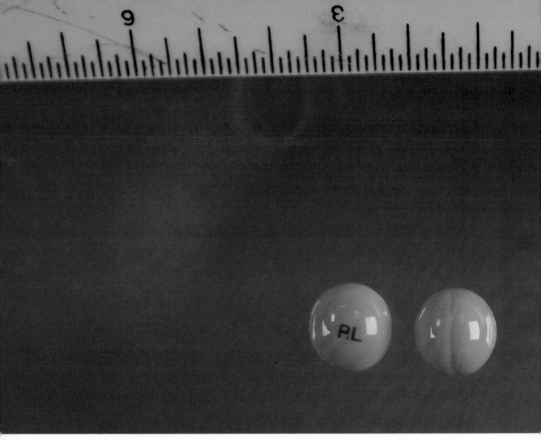

The FDA has not approved the use of marijuana for medical purposes. It has, however, given its approval to Marinol®, one of the synthetic forms of THC.

Like Elders, those who argue for the legalization of marijuana believe that not only is marijuana beneficial, it is also less harmful than many drugs we take every day.

Marijuana advocates also cite various studies that have proven the medical uses of marijuana. While some of these are private studies, three were done by the U.S. government, including a study done in 1999 by the Institute of Medicine, which showed the many possible medical uses of marijuana. According to these people's views, since even the government, the very organization trying to keep marijuana from being legalized, has proved its possible uses, marijuana should be allowed in certain situations.

Numerous polls have indicated that as many as 80 percent of Americans are for the legalization of medical marijuana. Meanwhile, many other countries have legalized marijuana in some way. In the Netherlands, cannabis is available by prescription in any pharmacy or drugstore. In Belgium, the government is considering allowing citizens to grow small plots of marijuana in their yards. Marijuana is currently decriminalized and somewhat tolerated. Marijuana is even provided by the Canadian national health-care service for medical use.

However, on the other hand, many Americans are against marijuana legalization. The official government position on marijuana states that there is no medical use for the drug and an extremely high potential for abuse. The FDA has not approved marijuana, which is reason enough for many people to not use it: if the FDA won't approve a drug, many people believe it too dangerous to use. There are, however, synthetic alternatives that are approved as prescription drugs. One of these is Marinol, which is synthetic THC.

Many people's arguments against marijuana are based on the ideas that marijuana is addictive, a gateway drug, and that the health risks are still unclear. Meanwhile, it is a known fact that cannabis can cause liver, heart, lung, and kidney damage.

Research indicates marijuana is useful for decreasing pains due to such illnesses as glaucoma, migraines, and even cancer. They also say that cannabis can decrease nausea caused by some forms of cancer treatment as well as *seizures* caused by epilepsy and even decrease problems due to depression and schizophrenia. Others, however, say that there is absolutely no medical use that is not far outweighed by the possible risks. This side is backed up by the U.S. government and therefore continues to be the loudest voice in the fight for the legalization of marijuana.

Other Proponents of Legal Marijuana

Some Americans believe that marijuana should be legalized for other reasons. The most important, for them, is simply that so many people use marijuana. Just as in the days of Prohibition, lots of Americans ignore the law, using an illegal substance recreationally because they feel the law is unjust.

Marijuana remains the most popular illicit drug of choice in the United States despite sixty years of criminal prohibition. According to the 2009 NSDUH, an estimated 104 million Americans aged twelve and older have smoked marijuana at some time in their lives. Of these, 28.5 million have smoked marijuana within the last year, and 16.7 million have smoked it within the past month. The vast majority of these individuals are otherwise law-abiding citizens who work hard, raise families, and contribute to their communities. They are not part of the crime problem, and some Americans believe they should not be treated as criminals.

Meanwhile, harsh federal and state penalties mean that marijuana offenders today may be sentenced to lengthy jail terms. Even those who avoid incarceration are subject to an array of additional punishments, including the loss of their drivers' licenses (even where the offense is not driving related), the loss of occupational licenses, the loss of child custody, the loss of federal benefits, and removal from public housing. Under state and federal forfeiture laws, many suspected marijuana offenders lose their cars, cash, boats, land, business equipment, and houses. According to some statistics, 80 percent of the individuals whose assets are seized are never charged with a crime.

Marijuana prohibition also impacts minorities more than it does white Americans. Blacks and Hispanics are overrepresented, both in the numbers of arrests and in the number of marijuana offenders incarcerated. Blacks and Hispanics make up 20 percent of the marijuana smokers in the United States, but they comprise over half of the marijuana offenders sentenced under federal law.

Nonviolent marijuana offenders often receive longer prison sentences than those allotted to violent offenders,

Even suspicion of marijuana possession can cause some people to lose their public housing residences. With many buildings having a long waiting list, many may be left with nowhere to go.

Members of minority groups make up the bulk of those incarcerated for drug offenses. This puts additional burdens on families and children.

and incarcerating marijuana offenders costs taxpayers. According to one pro-marijuana group, marijuana prohibition costs taxpayers at least $7.5 billion annually. The group states:

> This is an enormous waste of scarce federal dollars that should be used to target violent crime. . . . By stubbornly defining all marijuana smoking as criminal, including that which involves adults smoking in the privacy of their own homes, we are wasting police and prosecutorial resources, clogging courts, filling costly and scarce jail and prison space, and needlessly wrecking the lives and careers of genuinely good citizens.

The argument will not be settled any time soon. Meanwhile, however, the individuals whose lives have been damaged by marijuana addiction continue to look for answers.

 **Treatment**

Narconon Arrowhead is just one of the many program facilities designed to treat marijuana addiction. One of the facility's teen patients shared her story on MarijuanaAddiction.com:

> I really do not have the words to describe how I feel today as compared to the life I led engulfed in the degradation of drugs. How do you describe the day-to-day agony and humiliation of being a drug addict? Drugs control and destroy life and make you do things you would never dream of doing if not for the illusive and hollow promises you tell yourself that this chemical will give. How do you describe this insanity in such a way to make others understand just how devastating it really is? How do you explain a life without pride or integrity or peace of mind, not even a little? How do you describe the guilt and alienation from life?

Depending on the addiction, detoxification may take place in a hospital. Trained staff can ease the individual's withdrawal symptoms.

I came to Narconon Arrowhead a broken mess of a human being. I had lied to myself for so long that I started to believe there really was no hope for me, or a way out of the trap. I told myself that I was a drug addict and that somehow explained and justified my impeccably wasted life. I was more dead than alive and numb.

Today I have no words to really explain the difference in my life. The Narconon® program has taught me how to live again. Narconon Arrowhead has restored my faith in myself and given me a peace and stability that can only be dreamt of. No longer do the chemicals of evil men call my name or haunt my dreams. No longer do I fear or hate or have to hide. I am successful and happy and I have a future. I can see again and have restored faith in myself. I can look people in the eye and be proud. I can smile and enjoy even the smallest of simple pleasures.

Narconon Arrowhead made me whole again. How do you thank someone for saving your life?

There are many types of treatment for those who are addicted to marijuana. Some go through residential programs, like the Narconon Arrowhead Program, where they live away from home. However, people can also opt to attend outpatient recovery programs or attend group meetings like Marijuana Anonymous.

One type of drug treatment is outpatient drug-free treatment. This is often chosen when people have jobs or families and are unable to live away from home. The programs that these facilities offer varies; while some simply educate people on the dangers of drugs, others go into more depth and are closer to the residential programs in that they cater to a patient's individual needs.

Long-term residential treatment programs last anywhere from six to twelve months. Group therapy is often an important aspect of these programs, where patients live on a campus twenty-four hours a day and receive constant care and support. This treatment centers on developing a sense of responsibility and teaching residents new patterns of behavior that are not as destructive. This treatment option is not for everyone and is used mostly in the case of patients with more severe problems as well, such as mental disorders or criminal activities on top of drug use.

Short-term residential treatments are more intensive but more brief. They last anywhere from three to six weeks, but then are added to outpatient therapy and/or participation in a group like Marijuana Anonymous.

Medical detoxification is a process where drug addicts are withdrawn from the substance under a physician's care. It is not considered a full treatment, as it only gets the drugs out of a patient's system and does not stop the social behaviors that lead to drug use. Because of this, it is often used in conjunction with other treatment methods.

Principles of Treatment

The NIDA has come up with a list of thirteen principles that make up a good treatment program. These include:

1. No single treatment is appropriate for all individuals. Matching treatment settings, interventions, and services to each individual's particular problems and needs is critical to his or her ultimate success in returning to productive functioning in the family, workplace, and society.

For some users, treatment includes a stay in a halfway house. Many look like regular, single-family homes.

2. Treatment needs to be readily available. Because individuals who are addicted to drugs may be uncertain about entering treatment, taking advantage of opportunities when they are ready for treatment is crucial. Potential treatment applicants can be lost if treatment is not immediately available or is not readily accessible.

3. Effective treatment attends to multiple needs of the individual, not just his or her drug use. To be effective, treatment must address the individual's drug use and any associated medical, psychological, social, vocational, and legal problems.

4. An individual's treatment and services plan must be assessed continually and modified as necessary to ensure that the plan meets the person's changing needs. A patient may require varying combinations of services and treatment components during the course of treatment and recovery. In addition to counseling or psychotherapy, a patient at times may require medication, other medical services, family therapy, parenting instruction, vocational rehabilitation, and social and legal services. It is critical that the treatment approach be appropriate to the individual's age, gender, ethnicity, and culture.

5. Remaining in treatment for an adequate period of time is critical for treatment effectiveness. The appropriate duration for an individual depends on his or her problems and needs. Research indicates that for most patients, the threshold of significant improvement is reached at about three months in treatment. After this threshold is reached, additional treatment can produce further progress toward recovery. Because people often leave treatment prematurely, programs should include strategies to engage and keep patients in treatment.

6. Counseling (individual and/or group) and other behavioral therapies are critical components of effective treatment for addiction. In therapy, patients address issues of motivation, build skills to resist drug use, replace drug-using activities with constructive and rewarding nondrug-using activities, and improve problem-solving abilities. Behavioral therapy also facilitates interpersonal relationships and the individual's ability to function in the family and community.

Counseling is an important element of drug treatment. However, in order for it to be effective, the individual must want to be helped and do her best to work with the counselor.

The Twelve Steps of Marijuana Anonymous

The practice of rigorous honesty, of opening our hearts and minds, and the willingness to go to any lengths to have a spiritual awakening are essential to our recovery. Our old ideas and ways of life no longer work for us. Our suffering shows us that we need to let go absolutely. We surrender ourselves to a Power greater than ourselves. Here are the steps we take which are suggested for recovery:

1. We admitted we were powerless over marijuana, that our lives had become unmanageable.
2. Came to believe that a Power greater than ourselves could restore us to sanity.
3. Made a decision to turn our will and our lives over to the care of God, as we understood God.
4. Made a searching and fearless moral inventory of ourselves.
5. Admitted to God, to ourselves, and to another human being the exact nature of our wrongs.
6. Were entirely ready to have God remove all these defects of character.
7. Humbly asked God to remove our shortcomings.
8. Made a list of all persons we had harmed, and became willing to make amends to them all.
9. Made direct amends to such people wherever possible, except when to do so would injure them or others.
10. Continued to take personal inventory and when we were wrong, promptly admitted it.
12. Sought through prayer and meditation to improve our conscious contact with God, as we understood God, praying only for knowledge of God's will for us and the power to carry that out.

Having had a spiritual awakening as the result of these steps, we tried to carry this message to marijuana addicts and to practice these principles in all our affairs.

(Source: Marijuana Anonymous)

7. Medications are an important element of treatment for many patients, especially when combined with counseling and other behavioral therapies. For patients with mental disorders who have used an illegal drug to self-medicate, both behavioral treatments and medications can be critically important.

8. Addicted or drug-abusing individuals with coexisting mental disorders should have both disorders treated in an integrated way. Because addictive disorders and mental disorders often occur in the same individual, patients presenting for either condition should be assessed and treated for the co-occurrence of the other type of disorder.

9. Medical detoxification is only the first stage of addiction treatment and by itself does little to change long-term drug use. Medical detoxification safely manages the acute physical symptoms of withdrawal associated with stopping drug use. While detoxification alone is rarely sufficient to help addicts achieve long-term abstinence, for some individuals it is a strongly indicated precursor to effective drug addiction treatment.

10. Treatment does not need to be voluntary to be effective. Strong motivation can facilitate the treatment process, however. Sanctions or enticements in the family, employment setting, or criminal justice system can increase significantly both treatment entry and retention rates and the success of drug treatment interventions.

11. Possible drug use during treatment must be monitored continuously. Lapses to drug use can occur

during treatment. The objective monitoring of a patient's drug and alcohol use during treatment, such as through urinalysis or other tests, can help the patient withstand urges to use drugs. Such monitoring also can provide early evidence of drug use so that the individual's treatment plan can be adjusted. Feedback to patients who test positive for illicit drug use is an important element of monitoring.

12. Treatment programs should provide assessment for HIV/AIDS, hepatitis B and C, tuberculosis and other infectious diseases, and counseling to help patients modify or change behaviors that place themselves or others at risk of infection. Counseling can help patients avoid high-risk behavior. Counseling also can help people who are already infected manage their illness.

13. Recovery from drug addiction can be a long-term process and frequently requires multiple episodes of treatment. As with other chronic illnesses, relapses to drug use can occur during or after successful treatment episodes. Addicted individuals may require prolonged treatment and multiple episodes of treatment to achieve long-term abstinence and fully restored functioning. Participation in self-help support programs during and following treatment often is helpful in maintaining abstinence.

Marijuana addiction is a serious problem, but it's a problem that can be solved. The first step is to recognize the problem—and then seek help!

Glossary

bipolar disorder: A psychiatric disorder characterized by extreme mood swings, also called manic depression.

carcinogenic: Capable of causing cancer.

chronic: Long-term, or recurring frequently.

consensus: General or widespread agreement among all members of a group.

emphysema: A chronic lung disorder in which the air sacs are enlarged and lack flexibility, resulting in breathing impairment.

flashbacks: Later experiences of effects of a hallucinogenic drug long after discontinuing use.

gateway drug: A drug whose use is believed to lead to the use of other, more harmful drugs.

glaucoma: An eye disorder characterized by abnormally high pressure in the eyeball.

gout: A metabolic disorder in which excessive uric acid is produced and deposited in the joints, causing swelling and pain.

Great Depression: A drastic decline in the world economy resulting in mass unemployment and widespread poverty that lasted from 1929 until 1939.

hallucinogenic: Capable of causing hallucinations.

impunity: Exemption from punishment.

leprosy: A tropical disease that mainly affects the skin and nerves and can cause tissue change; in some cases, patients may lose their fingers and toes because of loss of circulation.

mandatory sentences: Penalties that must be imposed for a crime, regardless of circumstances that might otherwise influence the length of a sentence.

metabolites: Substances that are involved in or are by-products of metabolism, the body's breakdown of nutrients into usable form.

misdemeanor: A crime less serious than a felony with a less severe punishment.

neurological: Relating to the nervous system.

paranoia: Extreme and unreasonable suspicion of other people and their motives and actions.

pharmacopoeia: A book or database listing all drugs used in medical practice and describing their composition, preparation, use, dosages, effects, and side effects.

resin: A solid or semisolid natural organic substance secreted in the sap of some plants.

schizophrenia: A psychiatric condition characterized by a loss of contact with reality.

seizures: Sudden attacks of an illness or of particular symptoms, sometimes caused by an interruption in the electrical discharge in the brain.

sensationalist: Characterized by excessive emphasis on the most shocking and emotive aspects of a subject.

sterility: The incapacity to become pregnant or to induce pregnancy.

tender: Something that can be used as currency to buy goods and services.

yellow journalism: A style of journalism that makes unscrupulous use of scandalous, lurid, or sensationalized stories to attract readers.

Further Reading

Lawton, Sandra Augustyn (ed.). *Drug Information for Teens: Health Tips About the Physical and Mental Effects of Substance Abuse: Including Information About Marijuana, Inhalants, Club Drugs, Stimulants, Hallucinogens, Opiates, Prescription and Over-the-Counter Drugs, Herbal Products, Tobacco, Alcohol, and More*. Detroit, Mich.: Omnigraphics, 2006.

McMullan, Jordan. *Marijuana*. Farmington Hills, Mich.: Thomson Gale, 2004.

Mehling, Randi. *Marijuana*. New York: Chelsea House, 2003.

National Institute on Drug Abuse. *Heads Up: Real News About Drugs and Your Body*. New York: Scholastic, 2003.

Somdahl, Gary L. *Marijuana Drug Dangers*. Berkeley Heights, N.J.: Enslow, 2002.

For More Information

Brain Power! The NIDA Junior Scientist Program
www.drugabuse.gov/JSP/JSP.html

NIDA Infofacts: Marijuana
www.nida.nih.gov/Infofax/marijuana.html

NIDA Infofacts: Understanding Drug Abuse and Addiction
www.drugabuse.gov/Infofax/understand.html

NIDA Research Report: Marijuana Abuse
www.nida.nih.gov/ResearchReports/marijuana

NIDA Sites on Marijuana:
Marijuana, Facts for Teens brochure
www.nida.nih.gov/MarijBroch/MarijIntro.html

NIDA's pages on marijuana
www.drugabuse.gov/drugpages/marijuana.html

The websites listed on this page were active at the time of publication. The publisher is not responsible for websites that have changed their addresses or discontinued operation since the date of publication. The publisher will review and update the website list upon each reprint.

Bibliography

Anthony, J. C., and K. R. Petronis. *Early-Onset Drug Use and Risk of Later Drug Problems*. Drug and Alcohol Dependence 40 (1995): 9–15.

Bray, J. W. *The Relationship between Marijuana Initiation and Dropping out of School*. Health Economics 9, no. 1 (2000): 9–18.

Gfroerer, J. C., and J. F. Epstein. *Marijuana Initiates and Their Impact on Future Drug Abuse Treatment Need*. *Drug and Alcohol* Dependence 54, no. 3 (1999): 229–237.

Grant, B. F., and D. A. Dawson. *Age of Onset of Drug Use and Its Association with DSM-IV Drug Abuse and Dependence: Results from the National Longitudinal Alcohol Epidemiologic Survey*. Journal of Substance Abuse 10 (1998): 163–173.

Marijuana Anonymous. "Stories by Teens." http://www.marijuana-anonymous.org/Pages/teens.html.

Marijuana Anonymous. "The Twelve Steps." http://www.marijuana-anonymous.org/Pages/12steps.html.

Marijuana for Pain. "I Use Medical Marijuana!" http://tiffanyshay.tripod.com/marijuana4pain.

Narcanon of Oklahoma. "Student Stories." http://www.marijuanaaddiction.com/stories.html#student.

The National Center on Addiction and Substance Abuse at Columbia University (CASA). *Malignant Neglect: Substance Abuse and America's Schools*. New York: Columbia University, 2001.

The National Household Survey on Drug Abuse (NHSDA) Report: Marijuana use among youths. SAMHSA, 2002. Based on data from the National Household Survey on Drug Abuse 2000.

National Survey on Drug Use and Health 2004. SAMHSA, 2005.

NIDA for Teens: The Science Behind Drug Abuse. "The Lows of Getting High." http://teens.drugabuse.gov/stories/story_mj1.asp.

Partnership for a Drug-Free America Attitude Tracking Study, 2002.

Pope, H. G. *Early-Onset Cannabis Use and Cognitive Deficits: What Is the Nature of the Association?* Drug and Alcohol Dependence 69, no. 3 (2003): 303–310.

Youth Marijuana Prevention Initiative: The NCADI Report. U.S. Department of Health and Human Services, October 2002.

Index

addiction 13, 33, 61, 117
American Psychiatric Association 47
Anslinger, Harry J. 89, 94, 98
anxiety 57, 63
assassins 86

behavioral treatment 114
blunts 15
bongs 15
Bush, G. H. W. 24

Canada 24, 98, 103
conditional release 77
Controlled Substances Act 24
counseling 114

dealing (marijuana) 66
decriminalization 74, 77
depression 57
Diagnostic and Statistical Manual of Mental Disorders (DSM) 47
dopamine 57
DUID 66, 69, 70, 77

Elders, Jocelyn 99, 100

Federal Bureau of Narcotics 89
Food and Drug Administration (FDA) 103

gateway drugs 63

hallucinations 47, 54
hashish 13, 86, 89, 90, 91
health risks (of marijuana use) 36, 43–63
heart disease 54
hemp 13, 19, 70, 73, 82
history (of marijuana) 19–31

immune system 48, 49

Jamestown Colony 22, 82, 83
jazz 86
joints 14

legal consequences (of marijuana use) 65–77
legalization 98–107
lung cancer 53

mandatory sentencing 24, 74
Marco Polo 86
Marihuana Tax Act of 1937 92
Marijuana Anonymous 111, 116
Marinol 102, 103
medical uses (of marijuana) 73, 74
memory loss 57
mental disorder 47
mental health 54
method of action 15
Mexico 21, 24, 85, 86, 92
minorities (and marijuana use) 105
misconceptions (about marijuana use) 50
Mormons 85
munchies 45

Narconon Arrowhead 109, 111
National Institute on Drug Abuse (NIDA) 9, 10, 17, 112

outpatient treatment 111

Pancho Villa 85
paranoia 45, 54
peyote 23

Reagan, Ronald 24
reproduction system 58
residential treatment 112
respiratory effects (of marijuana use) 50, 53

sinsemilla 13

tax stamp laws 66

teens (and marijuana) 11, 36–39, 58, 63
THC 14, 15, 17, 45, 63, 103
treatment (of marijuana abuse) 109–118
Twelve Steps 116

withdrawal 63

Picture Credits

Comstock: p. 64
Corbis: pp. 25, 51, 75
Jamestown National Park: p. 82
Jupiter Images: pp. 8, 11, 12, 16, 32, 42, 46, 47, 52, 53, 55, 59, 60, 72, 76, 84, 87, 93, 105, 106, 108, 110, 113
U.S. Drug Enforcement Agency: p. 62, 80, 90, 102
U.S. Fish and Wildlife Service: pp. 21, 23
U.S. Library of Congress: pp. 95, 99
Young, Lisa F.: p. 115

Author and Consultant Biographies

Author

In addition to being an author and journalist, E. J. Sanna has a background in chemistry. She also enjoys traveling, music, and theater.

Series Consultant

Jack E. Henningfield, Ph.D., is a professor at the Johns Hopkins University School of Medicine, and he is also Vice President for Research and Health Policy at Pinney Associates, a consulting firm in Bethesda, Maryland, that specializes in science policy and regulatory issues concerning public health, medications development, and behavior-focused disease management. Dr. Henningfield has contributed information relating to addiction to numerous reports of the U.S. Surgeon General, the National Academy of Sciences, and the World Health Organization.